bulbs

JimHole Q&A

questions / ANSWERS

volume 6

bulbs

Practical Advice and the
Science Behind It

H||
HOLE'S

ENJOY GARDENING

Library and Archives Canada Cataloguing in Publication

Hole, Jim, 1956-
    Bulbs : practical advice and the science behind it / Jim Hole.
    (Questions & answers ; v. 6)

Includes index.
ISBN 1-894728-04-1
    1. Bulbs. I. Title. II. Series: Questions & answers
    (St. Albert, Alta.) ; v. 6.

SB425.H638 2005   635.9'4   C2005-900844-X

Printed by Capital Colour Press Ltd., Edmonton, Alberta Canada
Image on page 76 used courtesy of the Netherlands Flower Bulb Information Centre

---

HOLE'S
    101 Bellerose Drive
    St. Albert, Alberta Canada
    T8N 8N8

LONE PINE PUBLISHING
    10145-81 Avenue
    Edmonton, Alberta Canada
    T6E 1W9

Contents

Foreword
by Lois Hole

One of the things I love about my younger son Jim is that he genuinely appreciates it when someone asks him a question; to Jim, the process of discovery is just as important as solving any given problem. Jim's attitude towards customer questions is one shared by our entire family, and it became our guiding principle when we started publishing gardening books. As far as we're concerned, the books are not simply intended as reference works for gardeners; they also define and advocate a specific gardening creed: learn about gardening, seek out the best varieties, use quality materials, and above all, enjoy gardening.

I don't participate in the production of the books as much as I used to, but I still enjoy reading what Jim has written and offering the occasional suggestion or story, all in the name of making sure that our family philosophy never gets lost in the shuffle. Fortunately, Jim is as committed to that philosophy as I ever was, and more, so much so that I'll often pass customer questions straight to him if I have any doubt of the answer.

Over the years, Jim and I have answered a lot of questions, and given a lot of practical advice. I'm very glad that Jim's always been there to lend me a hand; we've learned a lot from each other, and we've reinforced each other's belief that good, solid information is the number one ingredient for success in the garden. I look forward to seeing him hand out some practical advice on his own, and to carrying on the Hole's tradition.

November 2004

My mother, Lois Hole, passed away on January 6th, 2005, just before this book was going to press. I'll do my best to keep her spirit alive in books to come, and carry on her tradition of providing practical advice to gardeners of all kinds.

Jim Hole
January 2005

The Q&A Series
Practical Advice and the Science Behind It

Bulbs: Practical Advice and the Science Behind It is the first book of the second phase of our *Q&A* series. It is the first full-colour book in the series, and the first without the direct input of my mother Lois. Instead of providing each question with an answer from both Mom and me, we've stuck a little closer to the subtitle and provided either practical advice, the science behind it, or both. As before, the practical advice—very much inspired by Mom's approach to problems—gives the reader a short but valuable answer to the question so that you can get right back into the garden. My forte, exploring the science behind the answers, provides more curious gardeners with extra facts and analyses that lead to a deeper understanding of how plants, the environment and human beings interact.

Bulbs also differs from previous volumes in the series in that it is very much an outgrowth of *Lois Hole's Favorite Bulbs*, published in 2003. After three years of research, writing and photography, we found that we had pages and pages of extra information, material that was too important and useful not to publish. But rather than double the size of *Favorite Bulbs*, we transformed that material into questions and answers for this book. Combined with your bulb questions, we feel that decision has made this our best *Q&A* book yet.

As we've said in previous books, success is built on a solid foundation of questions. No gardener should ever hesitate to ask a question, no matter how dumb or obvious it may seem on the surface. An innocent question from a new gardener in a unique situation can give even the most experienced professional a new way of looking at a problem and open up all kinds of possibilities for experimentation and discovery. A great gardener doesn't have all the answers; what he or she does have is an abundance of good questions.

Answering your questions—in this book, and all those preceding it— has been an incredible learning experience. You've forced me to find better answers, and as a result I've grown as both author and gardener. I hope you'll learn as much from exploring this book as I have in writing it.

Jim Hole

Acknowledgements

Thanks to the Netherlands Flower Bulb Information Centre, Toronto, especially Carol Cowan for her indispensable advice and information, and to our call centre staff, who dutifully recorded questions for our books even as they dealt with an incredible volume of calls.

Thanks also to those people who sent questions by e-mail to *yourquestions @enjoygardening.com*. Keep them coming!

Finally, thanks to professional growers and breeders, who bring us stunning new bulb varieties every year. You help make our gardens even brighter.

Introduction

Plants are complex, but gardening doesn't have to be. That's why I enjoy bulbs so much. For the past couple of years I've started tulips in my basement; all it takes is a couple of containers, some potting soil, water and the bulbs themselves. It's an easy task to plant the bulbs in the fall; I leave the containers in the cold room and take a peek at them every couple of weeks, watering them only to keep the roots from dehydrating. When March rolls around, I can tell from the strong green shoots emerging from those pots that the bulbs are ready and eager to go, so I haul the containers onto my deck and enjoy the show. What could possibly be simpler or more rewarding?

A Rational Approach

I admire bulbs for a couple of reasons. For one thing, they're simply fascinating life forms; all the energy required to create a flowering plant is stored in a relatively tiny mass of highly compacted plant parts, which lie dormant until they sense the time is right to resume active growth.

And yet, for all this elegant complexity, bulbs require comparatively little effort from gardeners to grow extremely well. Bulbs are very good at consistently producing very uniform plants; they can make even novice gardeners look like seasoned professionals.

The Business of Bulbs

We've been selling bulbs ever since we first set up our retail business in the early 1970s. Of course, the selection was pretty limited: just a few onion and garlic sets and gladiolus corms from our seed supplier.

Today, we sell over 800 varieties and species of bulbs, from the most popular, such as daffodils, tulips and crocuses, to more exotic bulbs, such as elephant ear, freesia and oxalis. We grow our own amaryllis for the Christmas season, and our own Easter lilies. And of course our perennial department raises all kinds of bulbs for sale as mature plants, most prominently lilies.

What I've always found fascinating about the business of bulbs is the incredible range of varieties the industry has produced—especially when you consider the number of failures it took to bring gardeners this impressive lineup of choices. For every new bulb variety that makes it to retail shelves there are countless that do not—known only to the professional breeders who developed them. The sheer scale of the effort that goes into producing the latest and greatest bulbs is a little humbling when you stop to think about it.

This End Up

Of course, home gardeners tend to have a different perspective on bulbs than professional growers do. And because bulbs are often touted as the simplest plant you can possibly grow, some gardeners are a little reticent about asking too many questions—particularly questions that seem like they should have obvious answers.

The most popular question remains, by far, "Which way is up?" If you've had any experience at all with bulbs, the answer is second nature: pointy end up or eyes up, or even root cluster down. But if you think back to when you first planted a bulb you'll probably remember that the answer wasn't all that obvious.

The number two question is really a series of related questions, all revolving around when to plant certain bulbs and when they'll flower—in other words, the whole spring bulbs vs. fall bulbs issue. Spring-planted, summer-flowering, fall-planted, spring-flowering…to be honest, when I was working on my mom's bulb book I got a little confused myself! I've come to the conclusion that what we need to remember is that these are all human concepts; to bulbs, no part of their life cycle, including blooming, is any more significant than any other part.

I appreciate questions from gardeners, and I think most professionals feel the same way. Questions aren't a sign of willful ignorance; they're a signal that the gardener wants to understand how plants work. And I respect intellectual curiosity probably more than any other human trait.

The Future of Bulbs

I think bulbs are going to become more and more popular as time passes. Many bulbs originated in extreme climates; the geophyte form (the proper, blanket term for bulbs, corms, rhizomes, etc.) evolved because plants needed a way to "weather the storm," to wait out harsh conditions and bloom only when the time was right. Many bulbs are some of the toughest plants out there, and they can play a significantly expanded role in North American gardens as we become more conscious about conservation. With a growing population continually stressing our natural resources, people are looking for ways to cut back on irrigation and reduce the use of chemical fertilizers; for these environmentally conscious folk, bulbs are the perfect solution.

Of course, there's a price for the popularity of bulbs: every season gardeners are confronted with an ever-expanding lineup of plants, a bewildering array of species and varieties to choose from. This "tyranny of choice" isn't limited to bulbs; in our consumer-driven society, we're faced with an enormous number of choices—everything from a dozen brands of toothpaste to hun-

Just how easy are bulbs to grow? The discarded tulips and daffodils in our compost pile are a testament to the resiliency of bulbs.

Imagine grabbing a fully grown plant—roots, stem, flowers and foliage—and squeezing it down into one highly compressed lump. That is a bulb.

dreds of makes of automobiles. Choosing the right bulb for your taste, your climate, and the conditions in your particular garden is going to grow steadily more challenging—but if you do your research, you'll be able to make the right choices.

The Structure of Bulb Gardening

There are two ways to look at bulbs: as plants that you tend to and admire, and as complex organisms to be studied. Different questions require different kinds of answers, so depending on the nature of the question, I respond with *Practical Advice,* which is just what it sounds like, or *The Science Behind It,* exploring the issues surrounding bulbs from a scientific point of view.

Generally speaking, Practical Advice answers give you hands-on advice that you can use right away, in the spirit of the answers that my mom used to give. In The Science Behind It, I take a closer look at the inner workings of bulbs, sometimes just so you can learn more about the science of bulbs, and sometimes because an answer may absolutely require a better understanding of bulbs' nature. Learning about the natural forces that shape the garden is, in my experience, the best way to enjoy better success with bulbs.

The book is divided into six sections that cover the most important fundamentals of planting, maintaining and enjoying bulbs. They are: The Basics, Choosing & Planting, Growing Bulbs, Enjoying Bulbs, Troubleshooting, and Species & Varieties.

A Living Legacy

Bulb gardening is an evolving hobby, thanks in great part to the myriad of new varieties we're presented with each year. Every passing season brings something new to try.

But we shouldn't ignore the genetic heritage of bulbs, the original species that provided the foundation for the hybrid varieties we take for granted today. It took millions of years for bulbs to evolve in the harsh environment of Asia Minor and in other inhospitable spots—hard-won experience that has created a remarkably adaptable class of plants, properly known as the geophytes: the bulbs, corms, tubers and rhizomes that give rise to a multitude of incredible flowers.

There are several sites around the world that store and protect so-called "heirloom" varieties: the seed of food crops and ornamental plants and bulbs of all kinds are kept in secure, sterile germplasm centres, facilities designed especially for the protection of these priceless resources. A team of professionals ensures that original plant species are not lost, but exist for our use, study and enjoyment in perpetuity.

Whether you choose to plant older heirloom species or brand-new hybrids, for my money bulbs offer the best cost/benefit ratio of any plant out there. For the practical gardener looking for a simple way to create a great-looking landscape, there's no better solution. So, with all the questions bulbs generate, it's good to know that they also provide plenty of answers for gardeners.

Fritillaria michailovskyi

1
the Basics

Bulbs are easy to grow, but to really take advantage of their special attributes you've got to understand their life cycles and the proper environment for growth. Spring-planted, fall-planted, spring-flowering, summer-flowering—it takes a little work just to understand when to plant certain bulbs, and when to expect them to bloom. But a good grasp of the basics will put you on the right path to a beautiful bulb garden.

Definitions

What are bulbs?

Practical Advice: Bulbs are plant storage organs that contain all the plant parts, including the flower. Imagine grabbing a fully-grown plant—roots, stem, flowers, foliage and all—and squeezing it down into one highly compressed lump. Under the right conditions, this compressed ball of plant parts begins to grow. Once leaves form, energy is diverted to new bulbs and the cycle continues.

Because all the plant parts are "built in" to each bulb, it takes a relatively small investment of money, time and labour for bulbs to put on a nearly foolproof show of colour. For the practical gardener, bulbs are a no-brainer.

The Science Behind It: Technically, a bulb is a type of geophyte, which is Latin for "earth plant." And that's a perfect description, because geophytes reproduce via underground buds as well as seeds.

Geophytes take several distinct forms: true bulbs, corms, tubers, tuberous roots and rhizomes. The geophytic form contains all the differentiated cells required to reproduce a complete plant, plus the food and energy necessary for that plant to grow; if you cut a true bulb in half, you can see the beginnings of the flowers and foliage.

Geophytes may remain dormant for months, but in the right conditions they grow rapidly because the whole plant is effectively compressed within the energy-rich bulb.

Gardeners may be referring to any geophyte when they use the term bulb, and we generally follow that practice in this book. In other words, a bulb, by any other name, produces the same result: a great show of flowers.

Because narcissus are true bulbs, the size of the bulb is directly related to the number and size of blooms produced.

Geophytes, or bulbs, come in a range of sizes, from the tiny Galanthus *to this giant* Colocasia *tuber.*

What is a daughter bulb?

Practical Advice: With many species, the true bulb that you plant in the fall dies after it has produced flowers the following spring. But the original bulb is replaced by one or more offspring, called daughter bulbs, which develop between the scales of the original bulb, known as the mother bulb.

The Science Behind It: The largest daughter bulbs are usually large enough to produce flowers the following spring, but the others are normally too small to bloom right away, and require another season of growth before they come into their own.

With the proper care and growing conditions, this pattern can continue for several years, until the clump of bulbs eventually becomes overcrowded.

But remember, not all bulbs produce daughter bulbs, or they may do so only irregularly. Daffodils and *Galanthus*, for instance, produce few daughter bulbs, and hyacinths and fritillaries produce daughter bulbs only after a few years of growth. Some families are simply more prolific than others!

What do you mean by "true to type?"

The Science Behind It: "True to type" means that the offspring are identical to the parent. Because nearly all cultivar bulbs have mixed backgrounds, the only way to produce true-to-type offspring is to harvest and grow any daughter bulbs the parent produces. In other words, you want to propagate the bulb via the asexual reproductive structures—i.e., the bulbs—not the sexual reproductive structures—the seeds. Bulbs that develop from the seeds of cultivar bulbs may have some characteristics of their parents, but not all.

15

Tulipa praestans is a reliable, hardy species tulip.

Gladiolus bulbs are sold in the spring—the same time they should be planted.

What are species bulbs?

Practical Advice: Species bulbs are non-hybrid bulbs, untouched by intensive human breeding efforts. They tend to be smaller and less showy than hybrid bulbs, but they may also be hardier and easier to propagate. (Which makes sense, because in nature bigger doesn't necessarily mean better. Big plants require more water and nutrients than small plants, so in an area with little water or food the little guys will out-compete larger plants.) Reliable species bulbs include species tulips, species crocuses, chiono-doxa, snowdrops, muscari, and scilla. All of these bulbs will produce reliably, year after year, and they will often spread across the landscape as the seasons pass, a process called naturalizing. If you don't feel like planting a new crop of bulbs every year, species bulbs are a great way to go; eventually, they'll create small waves of colour throughout the garden.

Species bulbs are best planted in small groups, in somewhat irregular shapes. They look great among rocks and on the slopes of a rock or alpine garden. The idea is to mimic the haphazard but elegant ebbs and flows of nature. And the best part is, it doesn't take much planning; often, you can just scatter a handful of species bulbs into the garden, plant them where they fall, and your neighbours will think nature did all the work.

Why can I buy some bulbs only in the fall, and others only in the spring?

Practical Advice: Bulbs are normally sold based on when they should be planted.

The Science Behind It: Bulbs purchased and planted in the spring are naturally tender, unable to endure the cold of winter; they need warm soil and sustained heat (and in some cases mois-ture) to bloom. Bulbs purchased and planted in the late summer and fall, on the other hand, are hardy. Not only can they withstand the cold, most require an extended period of cold to produce flowers the following spring.

Garden centres tend to carry products that suit the local climate. For example, while a canna lily may be available for fall planting in Zone 8, where it will survive the winter with protection, it is sold as a spring-planted bulb in the chillier Zone 3.

Q: Some bulbs are described as self-sowing. Does this mean the bulb reproduces itself or does it actually produce seeds?

The Science Behind It: Depending on the species, the answer may be both! All bulbs produce replacement growth during the season, whether that means producing daughter bulbs or enlarging the tuberous root. But some bulbs are prolific, producing numerous offsets each season. (An offset may be a daughter bulb, cormel or tuber.) Although the offsets are generally too small to flower in their first growing season, they grow, reproduce, and eventually produce blooms. Within a few seasons, a single parent plant may have dozens of offspring.

The Science Behind It: Many bulbs also produce seeds. Plants take longer to mature from seed and have a lower success rate, but some bulbous plants produce large amounts of seed. Between offsets and self-seeding, these plants may spread rapidly. When the term "self-sowing" is used, it is usually a caution—the plant in question may be more prolific than you wish it to be.

Calla lilies are sold in warm climates for planting in the fall, but in areas where they won't survive winter temperatures they are sold in the early spring.

Q: I'm a new homeowner with a lot of garden to fill. Some people have warned me against planting bulbs. Why? Are they really that difficult to grow?

Practical Advice: Ignore these people. Bulbs are among the easiest plants to grow! Sure, a few bulbs are finicky and require extra care, but most are tough and undemanding. If you're a novice gardener, plant some of the tried-and-true species, such as crocuses, tulips and daffodils. If you're more experienced, try more challenging plants, like bulbous irises, fritillaries and dahlias. If you want to fill the garden quickly, you can try mass plantings with spring-flowering bulbs like winter aconite, snowdrops, crocus, muscari, puschkinia and scilla, or go for height and volume with tender bulbs like elephant ear and canna lily. There are also bulbs, like allium (especially the smaller species) and snowdrops, which reproduce quickly and will fill their planting area within a few seasons. Bulbs offer so many options for such a range of planting situations that you're sure to find something right for your new garden.

The Science Behind It: That said, there are some common factors in new gardens that make growing bulbs a little more challenging than it is in established yards. Here are a few issues to consider.

- **Soil:** Some bulbs need soil depth of 20 cm or more. If your topsoil is new, how deep is it? Do you need to build up a bed for planting? What condition is the soil in, and is that soil well drained? Do you need to amend it with large amounts of organic matter? Are weeds a problem? Get the soil under control before you begin.

- **Moisture:** Have you determined the drainage patterns in your yard? Most bulbs are fussy about water, especially during their dormant period. If your tulips spend that period in wet soil, they're likely to rot.

- **Light:** If your yard is new, you're probably filling it with trees and shrubs as well as annuals and perennials. Bulbs have fairly high light requirements. As your trees and shrubs fill in and the sun/shade patterns change over the next few years, your bulbs may need to be relocated.

- **Movement:** Some bulbs don't like to have the soil they're growing in disturbed. Fritillaries and bulbous irises, for example, may need two or three seasons in a stable, undisturbed bed before they become established and perform well. If you're going to experiment and dig up your beds frequently, stick to species that don't mind some disturbance, or plant tender species that you can lift (or discard) in the fall.

Soil

Q: What kind of soil do bulbs prefer?

Practical Advice: Most bulbs grow fairly well in a range of soil conditions, including clay, loam and sandy loam. However, some require specific soil conditions to thrive. For example, Darwin tulips require rich, heavily fertilized soil to flower well year after year, whereas species tulips prefer leaner soil.

If you do your research and provide the specific soil conditions the bulbs require, you'll see much more reliable results in growth and flowering. This is why it pays to learn where your bulbs evolved. Many are indigenous to dry regions of west central Asia where the soil is thin and poor in quality; species tulips, for example, originated in Turkey. Hybrid tulips, on the other hand, were bred in Holland, a cooler climate with rich, deep soil, so they've lost some of their tolerance for hot, dry conditions. The species tulips are tougher in this regard.

Q: Why do you put sand in the hole with the bulbs when you plant?

Practical Advice: Actually you *don't* put sand into the hole, but you can amend heavy soil with it, if needed.

The Science Behind It: Although most bulbs tolerate a wide range of soil conditions, they are very intolerant of poor drainage. (There are a few exceptions to this rule, such as *Colocasia esculenta* and water cannas, which

If you do your research and provide the specific soil conditions bulbs require, you'll see much more reliable results in growth and flowering.

It is much easier to amend soil before you plant bulbs than to try and work around established clumps.

thrive in wet conditions.) Because of this fact, gardeners are eager to improve drainage, and according to popular convention, adding a little sand to the planting hole helps water to drain away from the bulb, preventing the bulb from rotting.

Unfortunately, the conventional wisdom is wrong. Sand in the bottom of the planting hole does very little. While it's true that water drains easily through sand, the water still requires a place to drain to; if the sand is sitting atop impervious clay, then the water has nowhere to go. Rather than adding sand to the planting hole, it's best to start with rich, deeply worked, well-drained soil in the first place.

Q: I have pretty good soil on the side of my house and it holds water well. But bulbs don't do well there. What's wrong?

Practical Advice: Pick up some soil and roll it around in your hands. If it stays in a tight ball and doesn't easily crumble between your fingers the soil is too heavy and lacks the air space roots need to absorb oxygen and the physical space to grow and for water to drain away. Amend it with organic matter to correct the problem.

The Science Behind It: Perhaps the problem also relates to *when* the soil is wettest. Is this the last area in your yard to dry up after the snow melts? Is it very wet in fall? If so, the bulbs may simply be too wet and cold to grow well, and they may even rot. Amend the soil or try growing bulbs in a different location.

Q: The soil in my garden is very sandy. Which bulbs are best suited to gardens with sandy soils?

Practical Advice: Pretty much all fall bulbs can be grown in sandy soil; try allium, gladiolus and *Crocus tommasinianus* in particular. Dahlias also grow fairly well in sandy soil, but they require extra care to ensure they have adequate moisture during the growing season. Extra mulch will help conserve moisture.

Q: Do any bulbs grow in poor, thin soil?

Practical Advice: Bulbs are tough, and many can be found growing in dry mountainous areas with thin, poor and sandy soils; they're adapted to it!

The Science Behind It: Indeed, the fact that geophytes evolved at all shows that their specialized storage organs were needed to endure the harsh conditions in their countries of origin. Species tulips actually prefer lean, gravelly soil. Many kinds of *Crocus,* including *C. crysanthus*, *C. etrucus* 'Zwanenburg', *C. sieberi* and *C. tommasinianus*, prefer coarse, well-drained, poor-to-moderately fertile soil. *Allium neapolitanum* grows best in sandier, well-drained soil, and *A. oreophilum* will tolerate poor soil. Of course, there's a difference between survival and thriving; generally most bulbs will do better in rich, well-drained soil.

Q: Do any bulbs grow in acidic soil? I'm thinking about the area under my evergreens.

Practical Advice: Although a few bulbs are tolerant of acidic soils, evergreens will out-compete any bulbs for moisture. Wood anemone grows well in acid to neutral soil but requires consistent levels of moisture. If your heart is set on having blooms under these trees, consider growing them there in attractive containers, provided that the area receives adequate light and the canopy is high enough to accommodate the containers.

Zones

Q: I transplanted some lily bulbs from my mother-in-law's garden in Toronto, but they didn't come up for me. What did I do wrong?

Practical Advice: The most likely problem is the difference between your zone and hers. Zone ratings are based on average minimum winter temperatures, but they also take into account other factors like the length of the growing season, rainfall, snow cover and wind. Toronto is in Zone 6a, a fairly warm zone. Within that zone, microclimates and winter protection in individual yards may allow gardeners to grow Zone 7 plants reliably—

and if the winter is unusually mild, even a Zone 8 plant may survive. If you're in Zone 5, a Zone 6 plant *might* survive the winter with protection, but if your location is in Zone 4 or cooler, a Zone 6 plant won't regularly over-winter successfully. That being said, don't be afraid to try out plants rated a couple of zones warmer than your own; the zones are just guidelines, and they're constantly being redefined.

Chilling Your Own Bulbs

If you're willing to give up refrigerator space, you can chill your own bulbs. Here's the method.

1. Put the bulbs in a ventilated bag. A mesh bulb bag, a paper bag with holes poked in it or a plastic produce baggie will work.
2. Set the fridge temperature from 4 to 7°C. Remove any fresh fruit from the fridge (fruit produces ethylene, which will interfere with the bulbs).
3. Keep the bulbs in the fridge for 8 to 15 weeks, depending on the variety. A longer chilling period is OK.
4. When spring arrives, plant the bulbs in the garden or in containers. When the flowers are finished, discard the bulbs.

Remember: vernalization is a requirement only for cold-season bulbs such as tulip, crocus, colchicum, muscari and hyacinth. Don't chill tender bulbs such as callas and cannas!

Q: I thought everything grows well in warmer climates. But in my zone I can't seem to grow spring flowers like daffodils and tulips. What can I do?

The Science Behind It: Most fall-planted bulbs absolutely *must* experience a long cold period in order to produce flowers the following spring. This process is called *vernalization*. After a number of weeks at near-freezing temperatures, chemical triggers within the bulb indicate that winter has passed and conditions are safe for the plant to resume active growth. Canadian winters make bulb gardening here possible. In very warm climates, the temperature does not remain near zero for long, and cold-season bulbs will not set flowers because they have not experienced vernalization.

If you want to grow cold-season bulbs in a very warm climate, buy pre-chilled bulbs or chill your own (see method at left). These bulbs have been chilled prior to sale; they are ready to plant and will quickly produce flowers. But remember, they will not set flowers if they overwinter in the ground because the climate is simply too warm.

2

Choosing & Planting

If you want to enjoy bulbs to their fullest, you've got to give them the best possible start. Know what to look for when shopping for bulbs, and what to avoid. Choose the best varieties, and then plant them in the right locations, at the right depths, in the right soil. If you start with a solid foundation, your bulbs will have little trouble reaching their full potential.

Choosing

Q: Could you explain the difference between spring-flowering, summer-flowering and fall-flowering again? When do I plant the bulbs for each type?

Practical Advice: Sometimes I even have to ask *myself* this question! Bulbs are tricky because we distinguish them in two ways: based on when they are planted and when they bloom.

- **Spring-flowering bulbs** are normally purchased and planted in the fall. They are hardy to most areas, although they may need winter protection in very cold zones. They emerge as soon as the weather warms up, sometimes even while the snow is still on the ground. Crocuses, tulips, daffodils and snowdrops are all spring-flowering bulbs.

- **Summer-flowering bulbs** are normally purchased and planted in the spring and are quite tender. Depending on their hardiness and your zone, these bulbs may overwinter in the ground or may need to be dug up and stored at the end of the season. Tuberous begonia, gladiolus and calla lily (a personal favourite) are summer-flowering bulbs.

- **Fall-flowering bulbs** are normally purchased and planted in the late summer; they burst into flower a few weeks later, just as the rest of the garden is finishing. These bulbs are normally fairly hardy and can be left in the ground over the winter (with protection in very cold zones). Autumn-flowering crocus and colchicum are the two most common fall-flowering bulbs.

- **Winter-flowering bulbs,** such as amaryllis and paperwhites, are purchased and forced indoors during the winter, rather than grown in the garden.

If you live in a mild zone with an early spring—such as Victoria, BC—the earliest spring-flowering bulbs may appear when the calendar still says it's winter! Galanthus and early-flowering crocuses regularly emerge in late February and early March in Victoria's gardens.

Shopping for bulbs in person allows you to examine the stock and develop an appreciation for the vast selection available.

Q: Where is the best place to buy bulbs, at the garden centre or through a catalogue?

Practical Advice: You can purchase high-quality bulbs at garden centres or through mail-order and Internet catalogues. At the garden centre you can examine the stock (a very important advantage if you aren't sure of the company's quality, or if you don't trust online or mail-order shopping), and you can choose your own substitutions if something is unavailable and ask for advice about planting or varieties. You can purchase fall-planted stock early and plant it immediately, giving your bulbs the best possible start. These businesses also offer bulbs suited to your local zone, whereas mail-order and Internet companies provide bulbs with a broad range of hardiness that may include all the zones in which their customers reside—this means you may have to do a little research to determine whether particular bulbs are suitable for your garden. Either outlet may also offer exclusive varieties or unusual selections.

Experience and word-of-mouth recommendations are your best friends in this regard. There's a wide variation in bulb quality from retailer to retailer; some companies sell small, immature bulbs that have little chance of blooming, and if they do bloom they may produce only a small number of flowers. Until someone you trust recommends a retailer, *caveat emptor!*

Small, immature bulbs have less chance of blooming; these big, plump tulip bulbs, on the other hand, are much more likely to consistently produce blooms.

Q: When I'm buying bulbs at a garden centre, what should I look for to ensure the best quality?

Practical Advice: There are five factors to keep in mind: firmness, weight, size, overall condition and timing. Healthy bulbs feel plump, firm and fairly solid, not squishy, soft or loose. They should be relatively heavy for their size. The outer skin should be relatively blemish-free and free of mould. Avoid bulbs that have visible cuts or bruises or that feel very light and dry. And of course, a healthy big bulb (within the limits of the species) beats a healthy little bulb. The most important tip is to buy early. Some bulbs, like fritillaries, dry out very quickly, so for best results purchase your bulbs as soon as they are available for sale and plant them immediately.

Q: If a tulip bulb has lost its skin, is it still healthy?

The Science Behind It: Some varieties of tulips shed their skins readily. As long as the inner flesh shows no bruising and is free from fungal growth and corky spots, it is fine. The area of the bulb that's most worrisome when it shows injury is the base (basal plate). Bulbs showing injury in this area will likely rot after planting. Avoid them. A healthy bulb should be firm, with no soft spots and no deep bruises.

Planting

Q: Is there a basic method for planting bulbs?

Practical Advice: Yes. It's simple.

1. Dig a hole to a depth of three times the bulb's height.

2. Put the bulb in the hole, growing point up.

3. Fill the hole with appropriate soil.

4. If you are planting hardy bulbs, leave a space equivalent to one to two times the bulb's height between large bulbs (5 cm or greater in diameter) and two to three times the bulb's height between small bulbs (less than 5 cm in diameter). If you are planting tender bulbs, space bulbs according to the diameter of the mature plant.

The Science Behind It: This basic method will produce healthy, attractive plants. Once you have mastered the basic method, you may start adjusting depth and spacing to accommodate your specific gardening needs or your own tastes. For bulb-specific advice, please see *Lois Hole's Favorite Bulbs*.

Q: I planted bulbs for the first time last fall and I just realized that I planted some of them upside down and others sideways. Will they still grow properly?

Practical Advice: Don't worry. Bulbs produce strong contractile roots that will eventually pull the bulb into its proper upright position. The newly emerging shoot will then grow upward.

The Science Behind It: The force of *gravitropism* helps plants reorient themselves regardless of how they land in the soil. Through the action of specialized structures within the plant, gravitropism ensures that root tissues grow down, into the soil, and stem tissues grow up, away from the earth. In some cases, a bulb will actually turn within the soil as the roots pull the bulb into correct alignment. But this work takes time and may consume the energy needed to produce big, beautiful flowers. For that reason, it's best to ensure your bulbs are set upright when you plant them and stay that way when you cover them with soil.

Q: What is bulb dust? How do I use it?

The Science Behind It: Bulb dust is a product that contains a fungicide and an insecticide, plus some inert material such as lime to "carry" the chemicals. These chemicals keep bulbs from rotting in the ground by protecting them from many soil-borne diseases and insects. Apply it by placing the bulbs in a bag, adding a bit of dust, and giving the bag a shake to coat the bulbs evenly. By the way, it's best to do this outside, in the garden, just in case you make a mess.

Q: The garden centre told me not to use bone meal when I plant my bulbs. Why?

The Science Behind It: For years, gardeners have used bone meal at planting time because it is high in phosphorous and promotes strong root development. Bone meal won't harm your bulbs, but it takes a long time for the nutrients in the meal to become available to the bulbs. There are other products available that may provide greater benefits. Try slow-release bulb fertilizer, which is formulated to provide optimum nutrition for bulbs.

Q: The garden centre sold me mycorrhizal fungi with my bulbs. What does this stuff do?

The Science Behind It: Mycorrhizal fungi are organisms that occur naturally in soil; they colonize the roots of plants, producing fine fungal root hairs (callled hyphae) and encourage additional root development. These tiny hyphae allow the plant to access certain nutrients-such as phosphorus-and moisture more efficiently, resulting in a healthier plant. Mycorrhizal fungi are sold live in powdered form. Simply apply the powder to the bulbs and the rooting area when you plant. If you fertilize your bulbs at planting time, make sure to use a fertilizer with less than 10% phosphorus, or use slow-release pellets. While phosphorus won't harm the fungi, it will reduce their ability to colonize the roots.

Which end is up?

This is probably the most frequently asked question when it comes to planting bulbs. With certain bulbs, such as daffodils, crocuses, hyacinths and tulips, it's fairly easy to recognize the pointed tip, that produces the growing shoot. With many other bulbs, such as anemones and tuberous begonias, it's not so simple. Here are some hints:

• Look for roots and the direction in which they grow away from the bulb. Roots usually indicate the bottom of the bulb. The side with the roots should be positioned down in the ground. Caladium and canna lily bulbs will often have some old roots attached.

• Look for shoots, buds and growth eyes. These growing points indicate the bulb's top side, which should be positioned upward in the ground. Gladiolus and tuberous begonia usually have small buds on their upper surfaces. *Colocasia* and *Alocasia* bulbs have growth eyes. If you're really unsure, use a magnifying glass to find the growing points.

• Plant the bulbs on their sides. It's not the best idea but it's a good second best, and the newly emerging shoots will know which way to grow.

• With begonia tubers, the rim end goes up. With dahlias, angle the tuber slightly down and outward. You can often see where last year's shoot developed when the tuber is set in the ground this way.

• With some bulbs, such as *Eranthis*, it's almost impossible to tell which way is up. In the case of very small bulbs, it just doesn't matter—simply set them in the ground at the correct depth and they'll grow just fine!

When to Plant

Q: When do I plant the bulbs I just bought?

Practical Advice: Plant your new bulbs promptly. Bulbs are perishable: they dry out quickly, and desiccated bulbs simply won't grow. Bulbs begin to grow as soon as they are in soil and although hardy spring-flowering bulbs don't normally produce top growth in the fall, they do develop roots. Get the bulbs into the garden so they can develop a good root system before winter arrives. In the spring, tender bulbs can be grown in a sunny indoor spot until the outdoor temperatures warm up.

Where to Plant

Q: What is a mixed border?

Practical Advice: A mixed border is a simply a fancy name for a flower garden that contains a mixture of shrubs, perennials, annuals and bulbs. Bulbs are an essential part of a mixed border. Spring-flowering bulbs, for instance, provide early colour and look wonderful tucked in among the other plants, which accent the bulbs in bloom. The other plants also help to conceal the dying foliage after the bulbs have finished blooming.

It takes a long time for the nutrients in bone meal to become available to bulbs— try slow-release fertilizer instead.

The Science Behind It: Just be sure to plant compatible species. For instance, don't plant thirsty annuals over bulbs that need a hot, dry dormant period. Also consider the plant size of the bulbs. Low-growing bulbs are better planted among low-growing ground covers and short annuals and perennials. Taller, larger bulb species such as dahlias, narcissus, hybrid tulips, gladioli and oriental lilies can be placed among larger plants.

Applying bulb dust protects bulbs from many soil-borne diseases and insects.

29

Q: What is underplanting?

Practical Advice: Underplanting refers to the technique of growing smaller plants at the base or under the growing canopy of a larger plant. Bulbs such as *Eranthis* look lovely massed beneath a birch tree, for example. *Colchicum, Eranthis, Galanthus, Leucojum, Muscari, Puschkinia* and *Scilla* are all suitable for underplanting. I wouldn't recommend underplanting under evergreens with lots of low, dense branches: they create too much shade and steal too much moisture for most bulbs to grow successfully beneath them.

Q: Are there any good bulbs for companion planting?

Practical Advice: Not really. Companion planting refers to the grouping of two or more plants so that one plant works symbiotically with the other. Bulbs don't normally form such associations with other plants.

Q: When planting bulbs along a wall or a fence, how much distance should I leave between the bulbs and the wall or fence?

Practical Advice: In general, I leave at least 30 cm between bulbs and a house, and 15 cm between bulbs and a fence.

The Science Behind It: I plant at least 30 cm away from the house for several reasons. First, the overhang from the roof creates a dry zone where rainfall rarely reaches. By planting bulbs a little further away, you can ensure that the bulbs enjoy the benefits of rainfall. Second, hardy bulbs planted close to the house may not overwinter successfully because the soil they're in is more susceptible to freezing and thawing. Finally, the sun's heat can reflect off the house and bake the mature plants. I plant bulbs closer to fences because the foundation and roof overhang are non-issues, and there's usually less reflection.

Position bulbs far enough away from buildings so that rain can reach them and where soil temperatures will remain constant through key dormant months.

3

Growing Bulbs

For the most part, bulbs are carefree, low-maintenance plants. But all bulbs need a consistent water supply and many will benefit from extra fertilizer. Some will need a little pinching or even require dividing after a few seasons of growth. Investing a little extra time in the care and maintenance of your bulbs will significantly improve their performance—and besides, part of the fun of gardening is spending time with your plants.

Sun and Shade

Q: What do you mean by the categories *sun* and *shade*?

Practical Advice: The terms "sun" and "shade" and so forth are used as general guidelines to help gardeners choose a location where a plant can thrive. Most plants, including bulbs, enjoy lots of sun, but some wither under strong light or prefer to keep their roots cool.

The Science Behind It: *Sun* means a location receives at least five hours of direct sunlight each day. By *direct,* we mean that the sun is high in the sky, normally between 10 a.m. and 4 p.m. *Shade* means that a location receives sunlight at a low, less intense angle before 10 a.m. or after 4 p.m.; it can also mean that the location receives bright indirect light. It does not mean that the location receives no light, because no garden plant can grow without any sunlight.

You may also see a few refinements within these broad categories. *AM sun* refers to the light received before noon. *PM sun* refers to the light received from noon until early evening. *Dappled sun* refers to direct sun that is relieved by intermittent shade, such as the shadows cast by tall, open-canopy trees. *Partial shade* means that a location receives some direct sunlight, but for fewer than five hours a day. *Dry shade* and *wet shade* refer to the moisture-holding capacity of the soil in a shade location.

Scilla siberica *prefers a location with sun to part shade. Scillas will not thrive in hot, dry conditions during the summer.*

Tuberous begonias do not like hot sun. They thrive in morning sun or 50 percent shade. Too much direct sun can scorch their leaves.

Note that AM and PM sunlight have the same intensity (assuming a clear sky), but that air temperature is typically higher in the afternoon: the latter is great for heat-loving plants, not so great for those accustomed to cooler temperatures. (Sun damage to plants is imparted by a combination of light and heat.)

Q: Are there any bulbs that grow in shade?

Practical Advice: Most bulbs prefer lots of light, but a few grow in less than full sun. Some bulbs that grow in full to partial shade are orchid pansy (*Achimenes*), wood anemone (*Anemone nemorosa*), tuberous begonia (*Begonia* x *tuberhybrida*), fancy-leaf caladium (*Caladium*), eucharist lily (*Eucharis* x *grandiflora*), pontica fritillary (*Fritillaria pontica*), blood lily (*Haemanthus*) and puschkinia. In partial shade try *Eranthis, Galanthus, Scilla siberica* and *Scilla mischtschenkoana*. The only tulip that performs well in partial shade is *Tulipa tarda*. Daffodils will tolerate some shade, but not deep shade and require at least half a day of sunlight to produce quality flowers year after year.

Remember that a number of bulbs grow successfully in early spring sunlight and may be located so that later, when their foliage is dying, they are shaded by the newly emerging foliage of trees and other plants.

Nectrascordum siculum *requires very well-drained soil and a drier location—specific conditions that create the best growing environment for this bulb.*

Water

Q: My gardening friends say that bulbs are fussy about water. What do they mean?

Practical Advice: Bulbs can be particular about moisture at specific times in their life cycle. Most bulbs should not experience wet, waterlogged soils while they are dormant or they will rot. While they are actively grow-ing, many bulbs also prefer loose soil that drains fairly quickly—they don't tolerate poor drainage. It's okay to saturate any plant with water, provided the plant doesn't sit in that water for an extended period of time. Think of it this way: a person can hold his breath underwater for several minutes, saturated all the while, without harm. But being saturated for an hour will undoubtedly kill him! There isn't much you can do about a rainy summer, but for best results plant your bulbs in well-drained soil. You may need to do a little research into the growing requirements of the bulbs you wish to plant in order to create the best growing environment. See *Lois Hole's Favorite Bulbs* for bulb specific information.

Q: I realize that some bulbs require lots of moisture when they are actively growing during the spring. How much is "lots"?

Practical Advice: Sometimes experienced gardeners will use general terms like "lots" when giving out advice, but we should really try to be more specific! During the spring growing season, many bulbs require about

1 to 3 cm of moisture every week. More than that is excessive, and if the ground becomes too moist or drains poorly, the bulbs can rot. Of course, this is only a general rule; the need for "lots" of moisture depends on many factors, including air temperature and soil type.

Q: Are there bulbs that don't require regular watering? I want easy-to-maintain plants.

Practical Advice: Yes, they're called light bulbs, and they really do "burn out" when watered! But seriously, some bulbs don't require regular watering, but even they may need help if Mother Nature doesn't provide adequate rainfall. Look for bulbs whose natural habitat is dry, such as *Allium neapolitanum*, *Allium oreophilum*, *Nectrascordum siculum* and species tulip, cape tulip (*Homeria* spp.) and corn lily (*Ixia* spp.).

The Science Behind It: To further reduce the time you spend watering, consider growing bulbs whose moisture requirements are high in spring—a time when rainfall may be frequent and the moisture from melted snow is still in the ground—and whose needs drop off as summer progresses. Bulbous irises and species daffodils are good examples.

Q: Should I mulch my bulbs after I plant them?

Practical Advice: I've long advocated mulching for several reasons, but especially because mulch helps conserve soil moisture. It also helps to keep the ground temperature even, prevents plants from emerging prematurely in the spring and limits weed growth. I prefer to use shredded fir bark or shredded leaves as mulch because they are airy and light, allowing air and moisture to reach the ground, and permit newly emerging plants to penetrate easily in the spring. Some people like to use straw, but I hesitate because straw attracts mice and other rodents and often contains weed seeds.

During the spring growing season, daffodils require about 1 to 3 cm of moisture every week.

Fertilizer

Q: Should I fertilize my bulbs when I plant them?

The Science Behind It: From a scientific standpoint, bulbs don't need any fertilizer at planting. They have no active roots and are thus incapable of absorbing fertilizer. As they begin active growth and develop roots, however, the need for fertilizer kicks in. So fertilizing at planting time is really a matter of convenience and simplicity, and not immediate need. And even though bulbs provide their own food supply, adding fertilizer will help provide bulbs with the energy they need to sustain growth in subsequent seasons.

At planting time, apply either a bulb fertilizer or a growth supplement (including mycorrhizal fungi) to encourage the development of roots. See page 28 for more information on mycorrhizal fungi.

Q: When do I fertilize spring-flowering bulbs?

Practical Advice: The first time to fertilize spring-flowering bulbs is at planting time, in the fall. Even though you don't see any above-ground activity, under the soil the bulbs are busily establishing roots to take up moisture and nutrients before they go dormant for the winter. Most bulbs also prefer a high-nitrogen feed (indicated by the first number on the fertilizer container) once during the growing season. Fertilize again after the bulbs have finished blooming in the spring. A general plan is to fertilize long-term, perennial bulb plantings at the end of the dormant season, just before growth commences, and again after flowering.

Allium oreophilum, one of the best 'old-fashioned' alliums, benefits from a good dose of water-soluble 20-20-20 fertilizer as the leaves begin to emerge and again when the flowers are blooming.

Fertilizer is available in slow-release and water-soluble forms.

Q: Should I fertilize fall-flowering bulbs in the fall or in the spring?

Practical Advice: Two principles come into play here: demand and convenience. Fertilizing at planting is easiest, but bulbs demand fertilizer most during the spring and summer. So why not do both? Fertilize bulbs like autumn-flowering crocus and colchicum when you plant (in the fall) and again the following spring or summer when the foliage is growing actively. This plan provides nutrients as the bulbs burst into bloom and develop roots, and again after dormancy when the bulbs are gathering energy to rebloom the following fall.

Q: Is it better to give bulbs liquid fertilizer or to top-dress the whole planting area?

The Science Behind It: Both methods have advantages and disadvantages. Liquid fertilizer makes the nutrients immediately available to the bulbs However, if the bulbs are planted in very fast-draining soil, some of the nutrients may be carried away. Top-dressing with a slow-release, granular fertilizer releases the nutrients over time; they aren't available to the bulbs immediately, but at least you won't lose as many nutrients to leaching. Top-dressing with compost releases nutrients slowly as the organic matter breaks down, and this process improves the soil's friability (ease of crumbling) and keeps it cooler and moister.

To fertilize naturalized bulbs, like these narcissus, sprinkle granular bulb food around the emerging shoots and water it in.

Q: I hear there are some bulbs that don't need fertilizer. That sounds good. What are they?

Practical Advice: That does sound good, doesn't it? Bulbs that prefer leaner, poor soils generally don't require additional nutritional support. A few examples include *Allium neapolitanum, Allium oreophilum* 'Zwanenburg', *Nectrascordum siculum*, species crocuses (*Crocus chrysanthus, C. biflorus, C. pulchellus*) and species tulips.

Here's another tip: if you plant certain bulbs—such as *Colchicum* and *Eranthis*—in rich soil, you'll notice they need little, if any, additional fertilizer. There are also bulbs—*Galanthus,* for example—that require fertilizer only at planting time.

Pruning, Pinching and Deadheading

Q: Do I need to prune or thin out any bulb foliage?

Practical Advice: Actually most bulbs don't requiring pruning or thinning with the possible exception of dahlias. Turn to page 97 for more information on pruning, disbranching and disbudding dahlias.

Q: What does it mean to pinch begonia seedlings? How do I do it?

Practical Advice: Pinching is exactly what it sounds like: using your fingers (or small scissors) to remove small amounts of young, tender growth—usually the end shoots. Pinching promotes stronger growth and more branching. It can also promote better and larger flowers.

The best time to pinch begonia plants is early in their growth. Pinch off stems that are too long or leggy. I like to keep the three strongest, most vigorous stems and remove the rest.

Q: Should I remove the flowers from my bulb plants after they have finished flowering?

Practical Advice: Leaving the old flowerheads on the plant reduces the size of the new bulbs produced, since some of the plant's energy is diverted to produce seeds. If you're growing tender bulbs that will be lifted in the fall, deadheading is a good idea.

The Science Behind It: If you're growing hardy bulbs and want your bulbs to self-sow, leave the flowerheads in place. Remember that hybrid bulbs may not produce viable seed; if they do, the offspring may not be true to type. It's interesting to note that although the offspring will definitely not be true to type if it is pollinated by another related plant, if there are no compatible pollinators present you have a fifty-fifty shot of producing true-to-type daughter plants: the seed produced will either be sterile, producing no plants at all, or true to type.

Leaving the old flowerheads on the plant reduces the size of the new bulbs produced, since some of the plant's energy is diverted to produce seeds. If you're growing tender bulbs that will be lifted in the fall, deadheading is a good idea.

39

After flowering

Q: I know I'm supposed to let the foliage on my true bulbs die back naturally, but it's been quite a few weeks and my garden is looking messy. Can I cut it back now?

Practical Advice: With true bulbs, it's always best to let the foliage die back completely. Once it is brown and dry, and comes away with a gentle tug, it's ready to remove. I understand how tempting it can be to remove it earlier, especially if the season has been cool and wet, and the foliage seems to be taking forever to die back! Try masking those ugly, dying leaves with some annuals or perennials.

The Science Behind It: It is crucial to leave the foliage attached to the bulbs because removing it prematurely means the plants may not be able to store enough energy in the bulb to produce flowers next year. However, if the leaves are completely yellow and beginning to fade, you can feel fairly confident about cutting them off a few centimeters above ground level. Use sharp, clean pruning shears, and don't cut too close to the ground so that you avoid damaging bulbs that may be growing near the soil surface.

It is crucial to leave the foliage attached to the bulbs because removing it prematurely means the plants may not be able to store enough energy in the bulb to produce flowers next year.

Wild crocus species propagate by seed. Crocus are propagated commercially by cultivating the young cormels that grow on top of the old corms.

Propagation

Q: Is it possible to grow bulbs from seed?
Why do we plant bulbs if we could just plant seeds?

The Science Behind It: You can certainly grow most bulbous plants from seeds instead of bulbs, but the results are much less reliable. Some bulbs take several seasons to grow to flowering size from seed—perhaps as many as seven years, or longer. During that period, the seedling is particularly vulnerable to diseases and pests. Some bulbs don't produce reliably fertile seed so you may have to start a large number of seeds before a seedling emerges. Perhaps most important, the seed of most hybrid plants produces offspring that are rarely true to type—in other words, you could go to a lot of trouble to produce plants that don't look anything at all like you hoped. (Seeds are like children: they share the genetic material of each parent, so they will probably produce plants that look similar—but not identical—to those parents.) Most home gardeners do not have the specialized equipment needed to grow these plants from seed. For all these reasons, it's much easier to grow these plants from bulbs.

Q: Do tulips produce seeds?

Practical Advice: Some species tulips will produce seed. *T. tarda* has particularly attractive seed pods. For those species that do set seed, removing the flower heads before they set seed allows all of the plant's energy to be directed to the leaves and photosynthesis, which will be channeled into the daughter bulbs.

Q: How are bulbs propagated?

Practical Advice: There are several ways of propagating bulbs, and several bulbs can be propagated by more than one method. The propagation method may be determined by the quantity of bulbs desired. Commercial propagation methods involve harvesting as many offspring or divisions as possible.

The Science Behind It: Some bulbs, tulips for instance, are propagated from offsets, the tiny bulbs attached to the base of the parent bulb. The bulbs are dug up after the foliage has died down, the offsets collected and replanted in the fall. It may take three or four seasons for the smaller offsets to grow big enough to produce flowers. Gladiolus is similar and is propagated by collecting the new corms, called cormels, which form on top of the old corm. These cormels are replanted in the spring and will not grow any larger, but about six weeks after the new shoot has developed the cormel will be replaced by a new cormel, which forms just above the old cormel, at the base of the stem. This new generation is known as a virgin corm. Virgin corms vary considerably in size. Many will be 2.5 to 3 cm or larger in diameter—large enough to produce flowers the following year. Others will require another season of growing before they reach flowering size.

For some bulbs propagation by seed is an easy method, but it's an awfully long wait from tiny seed to viable bulb. It can take more than five years for a daffodil to grow from seed to bloom. (See the previous question regarding growing bulbs from seed.)

Tulipa tarda is one of the few tulip varieties that set attractive seed pods, but it takes several years for a seed to become a flowering bulb.

Elephant ears are propagated vegetatively through slender stolons. Some species also produce smaller tubers (called eddos) that grow off the sides of the main tuber. These small tubers are the main method of commercial propagation and are typically separated from the main tuber in late winter or early spring. The tubers can be planted up in containers in colder zones or directly into the garden in warmer zones. Stem cuttings will also root very readily in water, especially in the spring and early summer. Dahlias can be propagated by nipping off and rooting cuttings taken from a newly planted tuber as the first shoots develop.

Chipping is a propagation method that involves dividing a bulb by cutting it into a number of segments when the bulbs are dormant. Snowdrops are commercially propagated using this method. Some tubers, such as begonias, can be propagated by dividing the tuber into sections. But division increases the possibility of disease or infection affecting the cut tubers. Dividing the tuber reduces its vigour, resulting in smaller plants. For these reasons, I don't recommend dividing begonias at home.

As long as narcissus bulbs are planted sufficiently early and sufficiently deep, they will withstand harsh winters and rebloom happily year after year.

Dividing and Lifting

Q: How do I know it's time to divide a clump of bulbs?

Practical Advice: A clump of bulbs will signal that it needs dividing by producing fewer blooms than in previous seasons or by not blooming at all. Some bulbs will even produce smaller, weaker leaves. With the right growing conditions, some bulbs, like narcissus, will grow successfully for years, even decades. They may need to be thinned every few years (three or four years in the case of narcissus) to ensure that they continue to bloom profusely, but if the clump has lots of room this may not be necessary.

Galanthus nivalis *is a bit different than most other bulbs in that it prefers to be divided after blooming, but before the leaves have started to fade.*

Q: When is the best time to divide a clump of bulbs?

Practical Advice: Most bulbs should be divided when the leaves turn yellow or immediately after the foliage has died back. Replanted bulbs need time to develop their roots before winter sets in. You'd be surprised how much help a little head start on the winter provides!

The Science Behind It: *Galanthus* prefers to be divided after blooming, but before the leaves have started to fade, and colchicum and crocus should be divided at bloom time or immediately after. Refer to *Lois Hole's Favorite Bulbs* for information on specific varieties.

Q: How do I divide crowded bulbs?

Practical Advice: Here is a general method for dividing bulbs.

1. Dig deep under the clump and lift it as a mass. (Large plantings can be heavy; you may need help.) Place the shovel several centimetres away from the growing area to avoid inadvertently cutting through any bulbs.

2. Gently shake off the soil and carefully pull the bulbs apart. If the bulbs still have foliage, work gently to keep the foliage attached.

3. Remove any dry, injured or unhealthy bulbs and dispose of them.

4. If the bulbs require it, add granular fertilizer or amend the soil in the planting area with sand or compost at this time.

5. Replant the bulbs at their original depth and spacing. Plant any extra bulbs in a new location or give them to other gardeners.

Q: I know fritillaries and bulbous irises do not like to be disturbed, but can I move them successfully if I am redoing a flowerbed? And what if the clumps become so crowded that they quit flowering?

Practical Advice: Some species are very slow to increase and naturalize, whereas others establish themselves quickly into large, robust clumps. These clumps will require dividing at some point or they will cease to produce flowers. The best time to divide is after flowering and just after the leaves have finished dying down, late spring for fritillaries and late summer for bulbous irises. Carefully dig up the clump, ensuring that you don't damage any of the bulbs. Place the entire clump with surrounding soil on a large sheet of plastic. Gently break away the soil and carefully separate healthy individual bulbs. Discard any bulbs that show signs of physical damage or disease. Replant the bulbs as soon as possible in their new location. Make sure you take the time to prepare the site properly before you replant. It will be a number of years before you divide again and you want to avoid disturbing them.

Q: How do I lift and save bulbs that won't survive winter in my area?

Practical Advice: Here is a general method.

1. As daytime temperatures begin to cool in the late summer, cut back on watering to encourage bulbs to go dormant.

2. Once the first frost has touched the foliage but before temperatures drop low enough to harm the bulb, dig up the clump. Be careful not to injure the roots.

3. Gently separate the bulbs by shaking away excess soil. If the bulbs do not come apart easily, do not split them. Do not wash the soil from the bulbs. (The exception to this rule is calla lilies, which should be rinsed gently with lukewarm water.) Discard any withered or bruised bulbs.

4. Allow the bulbs to cure for several days in a warm, sheltered location with good air movement, and then dust them with bulb dust. Store the bulbs in peat moss or vermiculite in mesh bags, nylon stockings, boxes or buckets in a dark, cool (but not cold) location.

Q: Can bulbs be lifted while they are still in bloom?

Practical Advice: We are asked this question when customers are moving and want to take their plants along. Unfortunately, lifting bulbs tears roots and sets the plants back, leaving them prone to stress injuries. It may take a couple of years for bulbs to recover from this disruption, so I usually suggest leaving these bulbs behind. Perhaps you can strike a deal with the new owners so that you can come back and lift a few bulbs at the proper time of year.

Many bulbs are aesthetically pleasing in containers because of their strong, upright foliage or interesting blooms.

Q: A friend of mine moves her daffodils and tulips around the garden each year and says it's really easy. That hasn't been my experience. What's the trick?

Practical Advice: If you want to move your daffodil and tulip display around each year or if you're planning to move and you want to take them with you, start by purchasing a shallow mesh container called a bulb basket. Most of them look like a round cake pan, but with a mesh bottom to allow water and roots to flow through. For fun, try one with an unusual, informal shape.

Half-fill the container with potting soil. Sprinkle granular bulb fertilizer on the surface and mix it into the top few centimetres of soil. Place a layer of bulbs on top. The bulbs should not touch each other—try to leave a few centimetres between them. Fill the container with potting soil; label for future reference if desired. Dig a hole in the garden large enough and deep enough to accommodate the container. Set the container in place and refill the hole with good soil. Water as usual. After the bulbs have finished blooming in the spring and the leaves have died back, lift the container out of the ground and move it to a new location. This is great way to experiment with different planting combinations each year.

Container Growing

Q: Which bulbs are suited to container growing?

Practical Advice: Many bulbs can be grown in containers, and the reasons for their suitability vary. Some are aesthetically pleasing in containers because of their strong, upright foliage or interesting blooms. Other bulbs need a jump on the season by being started indoors in pots that can easily be moved outdoors later—begonias, calla lilies, canna lilies, dahlias and elephant ears, for example. Many hardy bulbs like tulips, narcissus and scilla can also be grown in containers but require special care to provide the chilling period needed to complete their growth cycle (see below).

Q: How do I grow hardy bulbs (that I would normally grow in my garden) in pots?

Practical Advice: Containers planted in the fall with spring-flowering bulbs can look absolutely spectacular, providing an explosion of colour early in the spring. Keep in mind that bulbs in containers are less likely to over-winter than those in the garden because temperatures in containers get much colder in the winter than do temperatures below ground. You'll need to provide protection. Here's the method.

1. Sterilize containers before you plant to get rid of any disease organisms; dipping the containers in a solution of bleach is very effective. Use good soilless potting mix and not garden loam, which can become hard and compacted in containers.

2. Fill containers two thirds full—the bulbs should be placed about one third of the way from the top of the pot. Sprinkle a handful of granular bulb fertilizer on the soil surface and mix it into the top few centimetres of soil.

3. Set the bulbs into the soil so that they are spaced at least the diameter of the bulb apart and the same distance from the edge of the container. If you set the bulbs too close to the soil surface they may push themselves out of the soil as they develop roots. (If this happens, simply tip the soil out of the pot and carefully replant each bulb at a lower level. Be careful not to damage the new roots.) Do not allow the bulbs to touch each other.

If you live in Zone 4 or colder, move your container of spring-flowering bulbs into a cold room, cellar or garage where the temperature hovers just at or slightly above freezing. Once spring arrives move the container outside.

4. Water whenever the soil begins to dry out at the surface.

5. In you live in Zone 5 or 6, bury the planter in a leaf pile or in mulch until spring. You may also cover it with a frost blanket and peat moss, or even bury it in the ground. The ground acts as a heat source, which keeps the roots alive until spring. (If you live in Zone 7 or a milder location, this step is unnecessary.) If you live in Zone 4 or colder, move the container into a cold room, cellar or garage where the temperature is no warmer than 8°C but never much below freezing. Once spring arrives, move the container outside; I typically move my pots out in March. You can also bury the entire pot, turned slightly on its side, in your garden deeply enough to completely cover it with 10 cm of soil. (Keep the pot clean by wrapping it in burlap or plastic.) When the ground thaws in the spring, dig up and unwrap the pot, and set it in place.

Here are a few extra tips to ensure your success.

• Choose bulbs that are hardy to at least one zone colder than yours.

• If you're going to bury the planter in the ground, you can use any size pot you want.

Sometimes people ask if bulbs will rebloom in pots; they can, but few gardeners want to look at a pot filled with dead foliage during the summer. I prefer to discard these bulbs and fill my containers with fresh bulbs in the fall. If you decide that you are going to transplant the bulbs from the container to the garden (after the foliage has died down), remember after flowering has finished in the spring to feed the bulbs well with all-purpose fertilizer (20-20-20). It is also a good idea to mix in some more granular bulb fertilizer at this time.

Q: I planted my hyacinth bulbs in pots outdoors last fall. This spring the new shoots emerged and looked normal, but the plants never really developed. They just withered and died. What went wrong?

Practical Advice: Hyacinths are ideal for planting in containers, especially indoors, but they do not thrive in narrow window boxes and smaller pots that freeze completely in winter. Even if hyacinths are hardy in your area in the ground, they will be much less so in containers. The earth is a massive heat source and can keep the bulbs warm even in the face of frost; the soil in containers just isn't warm enough to do that. I'd advise you to plant hyacinths directly into the garden, but if you're set on growing them in containers dig those pots into the ground in the fall so that the earth will help insulate them over the winter.

Q: I'm growing bulbs in containers. How much water do they need?

Practical Advice: As a family, we're big advocates of container gardening, and our yards are full of planters. However, they do require a bit of extra maintenance because, in general, containers require more frequent watering than beds.

The Science Behind It: How much water the plants need depends on the type of bulb, its specific moisture needs, the size of the container and the type of soil. The container's location may also affect how frequently you need to water; if your pot is in a very hot, sunny location it will obviously dry out much faster than one in a cooler, shadier spot. In general, the soil in the container should be evenly moist, not wet. Check the soil several times a week; in very hot weather, you may need to check daily.

If the soil is well-drained, you can simply water the containers until the soil is completely saturated, then let the soil dry down to the point that the plants themselves look just a bit dry. Repeat this cycle throughout the season. Remember, the bigger the container, the more water is required to irrigate your plants thoroughly.

Dahlias are easily grown in pots, but must be kept watered and fertilized.

Combine geraniums, petunias and canna lilies for a stunning container display.

Q: Should I use fertilizer on bulbs grown in containers?

Practical Advice: Yes. Bulbs planted in containers have less soil volume to draw nutrients from, so adding fertilizer is important to achieve the best growth and flower development.

Q: Can I plant crocuses in containers?

Practical Advice: Yes, but I wouldn't recommend it. Most crocus bulbs (with the exception of the larger-flowered yellow varieties) are hardy and can survive in containers in areas where the winters are not too severe. However, the flowers don't last long; it's a lot of work for a brief display. Personally, I prefer to plant crocuses in the ground.

Q: What are the best daffodil varieties for container planting?

Practical Advice: You have a fairly wide range of options, but stick with hardy varieties to ensure success. Cultivars from the small-cupped, large-cupped, poeticus, trumpet, split-corona, double and botanical divisions are suitable.

I prefer to plant one variety per container for maximum impact. Although planting a number of varieties produces a longer blooming period, the later flowers will be set against the dying foliage of the early bloomers, which somewhat dilutes the impact of the new blooms. If you do wish to plant more than one variety/bulb type in your containers, choose varieties that have similar flowering periods.

Q: One of my friends plants these beautiful containers of bulbs that seem to bloom for months. What's the secret?

Practical Advice: Your friend may be using a technique called layered planting. Bulbs are planted in layers (like a lasagna), and the blooms are presented in succession for an extended period. Your friend may also be planting bulbs with long blooming periods in combination with annuals (cannas with petunias, for example). Give it a try yourself, and I bet you'll enjoy blooms for as long as your neighbour—just don't tell her we gave away the secret!

4
Enjoying Bulbs

There are many ways to enjoy bulbs; for me, it's a simple matter of taking in the sight of the huge pot of cannas on my deck. Others may prefer the effect of tulips or narcissus naturalized in grass, or hyacinths grown indoors. Many bulbs produce excellent cutflowers, and some gardeners grow them specifically for harvesting. But it's important to note that the key to getting the most out of your bulbs is to understand their potential. Get to know your bulbs, and they'll provide plenty of enjoyment.

Naturalizing

Q: What is a naturalized bulb planting?
Can I do this in my yard?

Practical Advice: The term *naturalized* refers to plants that are grown in locations, numbers and arrangements that simulate natural settings, supposedly unplanned and largely untended by the gardener. In other words, nature does the work! One advantage of bulbs suited to naturalizing is that they require very little care. They increase by means of both division and self-seeding but do not spread so rapidly that they crowd out other plants, a problem with some perennials.

The objective of a naturalized bulb planting is to create a display that looks as if the plants grew on their own. This look can be achieved by following two rules. First, avoid using too many species in one area. (This rule includes using too many varieties of a single species in one area.) Second, avoid planting the bulbs in a regular or geometric arrangement—after all, you don't often find perfect squares or triangles in nature.

The objective of a naturalized bulb planting is to create a display that looks as if the plants grew on their own.

Plant bulbs in small, odd-numbered clumps or in massed drifts with rough edges. The spacing between plantings should be irregular, not predictable, and each planting can be a different size and shape—think of meadows of flowers or the forest understorey as models. A naturalized planting is meant to last for years; it will expand and change each season in response to garden conditions.

Q: Which hybrid tulips are best suited to naturalizing?

The Science Behind It: Species tulips naturalize best because they almost always reproduce true to type, but some hybrid varieties also naturalize fairly well. Choose botanical tulips and their hybridized strains. These bulbs have not been extensively crossbred and are closer to those found in nature.

The key to naturalizing hybrid tulips successfully is choosing a location with very well-drained soil. Plant the bulbs deeper than you normally would: 1½ to 2 times the recommended depth. (The added depth will provide additional protection against rodents, temperature fluctuations and moisture loss.) Here are some varieties to try.

T. praestans
 'Fusilier'

T. kaufmanniana
 'Heart's Delight'
 'Showwinner'
 'Stresa'

T. fosteriana
 'Candela'
 'Madame Lefeber'
 'Orange Emperor'
 'Princeps'
 'Purissima'

T. greigii
 'Plaisir'
 'Toronto'

Single early varieties
 'Charles'
 'Christmas Marvel'
 'Coleur Cardinal'

Double early varieties
 'Peach Blossom'

Triumph varieties
 'Abu Hassan'
 'Don Quichotte'
 'Golden Melody'
 'Kees Nelis'
 'Peerless Pink'
 'Princess Irene'

Darwin hybrids
 'Apeldoorn'
 'Beauty of Apeldoorn'
 'Golden Apeldoorn'
 'Oxford'

Lily-flowered varieties
 'Aladdin'
 'Ballade'
 'Maytime'
 'White Triumphator'

Fringed varieties
 'Arma'
 'Burgundy Lace'

Parrot varieties
 'Estella Rijnveld'

Double late varieties
 'Angelique'

T. kaufmanniana
'Heart's Delight'

53

Q: Which daffodils naturalize well?

The Science Behind It: Species narcissus are well suited to naturalizing. Several cultivars also naturalize well. Here's a list.

Small-cupped cultivars
'Actaea'
'Barrett Browning'
'Birma'

Large-cupped cultivars
'Carlton'
'Flower Record'
'Fortune'
'Ice Follies'
'Salome'

Botanical daffodils
'February Gold'
'Hawera'
'Jack Snipe'
'Minnow'
'Peeping Tom'
'Suzy'
'Tête à Tête'

Trumpet daffodils
'Mount Hood'

Q: I want to plant spring-flowering bulbs in my lawn. Is this hard to do?

Practical Advice: No, but it requires some planning. The most important consideration is that you can't cut your lawn until the bulb foliage has died back, approximately six weeks after flowering. If you are prepared to live with long grass for a while, here's what to do.

Botanical daffodil 'Jack Snipe' is a great choice for naturalizing in grass.

To keep naturalized plantings growing well, sprinkle granular bulb food around the newly emerging shoots.

Gently scatter the bulbs across the grass and plant them where they fall to achieve a natural effect. Crocus, which look lovely planted in a lawn, are planted most effectively 125 to 150 corms per square metre. The easiest varieties to grow are those that self-propagate readily, such as *C. tommasinianus* and *C. chrysanthus*. *C. vernus* also grows well in lawns, but it spreads less readily and flowers a bit later. Yellow varieties are the best choice because the yellow flowers contrast so beautifully with the emerald green of the lawn. If you're really fond of blue and purple crocuses, then I would advise mixing them with other colours.

I also recommend small narcissus hybrids for naturalizing in lawn, particularily *N. cyclamineus* hybrids such as 'Jack Snipe', 'Beryl' or 'Little Witch' and *N. triandrus* hybrids such as 'Thalia' and 'Tresamble'. The botanical narcissus *N. pseudonarcissus* is also an excellent choice, but it will be slower to settle in and sometimes requires a couple of seasons before it becomes well established.

Q: I planted bulbs in the lawn but they didn't grow. What went wrong?

Practical Advice: If your bulbs don't emerge through the grass in the spring, it may indicate that the turf is too dense. This problem can be fixed by removing the turf directly above the bulb and then plugging the hole with good compost or potting soil. The grass will eventually regrow over the plug, but by that time the bulbs will be well established and won't have any difficulty emerging through the lawn.

The spacing between naturalized plantings, whether in lawns or in beds, should be irregular, not predictable, and each planting can be a different size and shape—think of meadows of flowers or the forest understorey as models.

Q: Can colchicum be naturalized in grass?

Practical Advice: Yes, but it's a little tricky. The timing of the grass cutting is critical. You must make the last cut around the end of August, just as the flower buds are beginning to peek through the ground. Set the blade high enough to avoid damaging these buds. You also have to check daily to determine the stage of the colchicums. Once they begin to flower, they emerge quickly and a few days of warm weather could make the difference between flowers emerging and blooming.

Cutting the lawn in the spring is also an issue. Although colchicum blooms in the fall, the leaves emerge in the spring and must be allowed to grow and die back on their own in order to replenish the bulbs. The leaves last for six or seven weeks—six or seven weeks during which you will not be able to cut your lawn, at least not in the area where the colchicums are planted. Finally, a legitimate excuse not to mow the lawn!

Q: Last year I used bulbs in a naturalized planting. Should I fertilize them? How?

Practical Advice: Yes. To keep your bulbs growing well, give them some fertilizer each spring. Sprinkle granular bulb food around the newly emerging shoots and water it in. You can also top dress the area with a thin layer of compost early in the spring.

Forcing

Q: I've seen pictures of flowering bulbs grown indoors in water. How is it done?

Practical Advice: Bulbs are just highly compressed plants, and so they're kind of like Sea Monkeys: just add water and watch them grow! Getting bulbs to bloom indoors is known as *forcing*, and it is done in two ways: in soil and in water. Regardless of which method you use, purchase firm, unblemished bulbs. Prepared or pre-chilled bulbs have been specially cooled. This treatment is used on bulbs to be forced indoors or for commercially-grown bulbs used as cutflowers. The varieties chosen are especially suited to forcing.

Paperwhites, amaryllis and pre-chilled hyacinths are among the most commonly forced bulbs. Here is a general method for forcing in water.

1. Use a forcing vase or any narrow-necked vase that will support the bulb over the water.

2. Fill the vase with water and position a bulb in the vase. Be sure the base of the bulb is close to the water level but not touching the water.

3. Put the vase in a cool but sunny spot. Roots should start to develop within a few days, but flowers take at least a couple of weeks to appear. Keep the water level high—just below the base of the bulb. And change the water frequently because it will get slimy fairly quickly.

4. Once the flowers have appeared, display the vase anywhere you wish.

Pre-chilled hyacinth bulbs can be forced to flower indoors in water or soil.

Best bulbs for forcing

amaryllis
colchicum
crocus
daffodils
freesia
hyacinth
Iris reticulata
muscari
paperwhites
tulips

Some bulbs, including tulips, crocuses, daffodils, bulbous irises, muscari and many lilies, are better forced in soil. Here is one method.

1. Fill a 15-cm pot with 3 cm of soilless mix. Be sure the pot has drainage holes and use high-quality soilless mix.

2. Place several bulbs on the soil, but don't let them touch each other. Cover the bulbs with soil to fill the pot to within 3 cm of the top.

3. Water the pot well and let the bulbs root for several weeks at 20°C or so. Then, store the pot in a refrigerator or root cellar at 4–10°C. (Keep the pot away from fruit. Some fruit, such as apples and peaches, releases ethylene that may damage the bulb.)

4. After about 16 weeks, place the pot near a bright and sunny, but cool window. Shoots will emerge in a few weeks, followed shortly by flowers. Water the bulbs sparingly; let the edges of the soil dry out before each watering.

Remember that bulbs forced indoors and left indoors tend to get soft and are very difficult to reforce the following year. When the flowers have finished, you can try planting the bulbs in the garden.

Best crocus varieties for forcing

'Flower Record' • Violet-mauve

'Jeanne d'Arc' • Pure white with deep-purple stripes

'Pickwick' • Amethyst-violet with lighter stripes

'Remembrance' • Deep blue-violet with silvery stripes

Crocus vernus
'Remembrance'

Crocus vernus 'Flower Record'

Trumpet narcissus 'Dutch Master'

How to Force Daffodils Indoors

Forcing daffodils indoors is easy, and the flowers produce wonderful colour during a sometimes drab season.

1. In the fall, plant daffodils in pots using good-quality all-purpose potting mix—no fertilizer is required. Ensure the mix is moist at all times but never wet or soggy.
2. Daffodils require at least twelve weeks of cold temperatures. For a minimum of six weeks keep them in an unheated garage or, if the container is small enough, in the fridge (remove any ethylene producing fruit first).
3. After at least six weeks of chilling, put the pot in the coolest room of your house. Light isn't a factor until the new shoots begin to emerge.
4. Once the shoots emerge (usually in a few weeks), bring the pot to room temperature and provide good light. You will soon have a beautiful pot of flowering daffodils.

For best results, use only varieties suitable for forcing. As a rule, early-flowering cultivars force easily and reliably.

Best narcissus varieties for forcing

'Ballade' • White; tall, may require staking
'Barrett Browning' • White with orange corona
'Bridal Crown' • White with orange corona
'Brighton' • Yellow; tall, may require staking
'Carlton' • Yellow; tall, may require staking
'Cassata' • White with yellow corona
'Cragford' • Yellow
'Dutch Master' • Yellow; tall, may require staking
'Easter Joy' • Yellow
'Flower Drift' • White with orange and yellow corona
'Geranium' • White with orange corona
'Gold Medal' • Yellow
'Golden Bells' • Yellow
'Golden Harvest' • Yellow
'Ice Follies' • White; tall, may require staking
'Jetfire' • Yellow with orange corona
'Little Gem' • Yellow
'Mount Hood' • White
Paperwhite 'Ziva' • White
'Pinza' • Yellow with orange corona
'Primeur' • White
'Quince' • Yellow
'Salome' • White with pink and yellow corona
'Sir Winston Churchill' • White with orange corona
'Tête à Tête' • Yellow
'Topolino' • Yellow
'Van Sion' • Yellow

Hyacinth 'City of Haarlem' makes a great choice for forcing.

Forcing amaryllis

Although most bulbs cannot be reforced after blooming indoors, amaryllis is an exception. With proper care, amaryllis bulbs can be forced repeatedly. Here's the method.

1. After the bulb has finished flowering (typically in the late winter or early spring), cut off the flower stalk very close to the base.
2. Keep the plant moist and feed regularly with houseplant fertilizer. The plant must be kept in a sunny spot.
3. In August/September, stop watering and feeding the plant. Allow it to dry out completely.
4. Dig up the bulbs and remove dead foliage and old scales. Check the root carefully—it should be full and fleshy. If it is damaged, it is unlikely to regrow.
5. Replant the bulb in a clean container. Leave the neck of the bulb above the soil surface. Water the container and place it in a cool, sunny location.
6. Water the container sparingly until the first shoot appears, and then keep the soil moist. The bulb will bloom about eight weeks later. I left mine in a pot and it rebloomed many times!

Best hyacinth varieties for forcing

'Amsterdam' • Deep red
'Anna Liza' • Mauve
'Anna Marie' • Pale pink
'Atlantic' • Blue
'Blue Jacket' • Violet
'Blue Star' • Lilac-blue
'Carnegie' • White
'City of Haarlem' • Soft yellow
'Delft Blue' • Soft lilac-blue
'Jan Bos' • Spiraea-red
'King of the Blues' • Indigo
'L'Innocence' • Ivory-white
'Lady Derby' • Pale pink
'Marconi' • Deep pink
'Pink Pearl' • Brilliant bright pink
'Splendid Cornelia' • Pastel lilac

Greigii tulip 'Pinocchio'

Best tulips for forcing

Tulips need 14 to 20 weeks of chilling (depending on the variety) and 2 to 3 weeks at indoor temperatures before coming into flower.

'Abba' • Red

'Abra' • Dark red with yellow edges

'All Seasons' • Cherry red

'Angelique' • Blush pink

'Annie Schilder' • Rosy orange

'Arabian Mystery' • Purple with white edges

'Arie Hoek' • Red

'Arma' • Red with fringes

'Barcelona' • Violet

'Bastogne' • Red

'Blenda' • Carmine-red with white base

'Capri' • Cardinal red with carmine edges

'Carola' • Dark pink

'Cassini' • Blood-red

'Christmas Dream' • Rosy-red

'Couleur Cardinal' • Violet-red

'Debutante' • Cherry-red with white edges

'Esther' • Fuchsia-pink

'Flair' • Red

'Friso' • Red

'Globe' • Dark pink

'Hollandia' • Vermilion

'Inzell' • Ivory-white

'Kareol' • Deep golden-yellow

'Kees Nelis' • Red with yellow edge

'Leen van der Mark' • Red with white edges

'Leo Visser' • Light red with white edge

'Libretto' • Rose

'Madison Garden' • Carmine with pink edges

'Merry Christmas' • Red

'Monsella' • Yellow with red flame

'Monte Carlo' • Lemon-yellow

'Montreux' • Primrose-yellow blushed pink

'Negrita' • Deep purple

'Orange Cassini' • Orange

'Orange Monarch' • Orange

'Oscar' • Red

'Page Polka' • Deep red with white stripe

'Passionale' • Purple

'Peach Blossom' • Carmine pink with white base

'Peach Blossom' • Tender pink

'Pinocchio' • Scarlet with ivory-white edge

'Plaisir' • Carmine-red with yellow edges

'Prinscess Irene' • Orange with purple flames

'Princess Victoria' • Pale red with white edges

'Purple Prince' • Purple-violet

'Recreado' • Magenta

'Red Paradise' • Vermilion

'Red Present' • Dark red

'Red Riding Hood' • Carmine-red with yellow edges

'Rococo' • Carmine-red with fire-red edges

'Rosario' • Rose with white base

'Sevilla' • Red

'Stockholm' • Scarlet with yellow

'Topwhite' • White

'Upstar' • Ivory-white with rosy-purple edges

'Van Eijk' • Salmon

'Viking' • Red with flames

'White Dream' • Ivory-white

'Wirosa' • Pink with white edges

'Yellow Flight' • Yellow

'Yellow Present' • Creamy-yellow

'Yokohama' • Lemon-yellow

Anemone coronaria *'The Governor'*

Bulbs as Cutflowers

Q: Which flowering bulbs make good cutflowers?

Practical Advice: Probably the two most commonly used bulbs for cutflower bouquets are daffodils and tulips, but there are certainly more choices available. Poppy anemone (*Anemone coronaria*), freesias, hyacinths, Oriental lilies, muscari, paperwhites and scillas are all fragrant options, but truly, any flowering bulb can be used (with the exception of a few that may be rather unpleasant smelling, such as *Allium moly* or *Fritillaria imperialis*). Use *Allium aflatunense*, *A. cernuum*, *A. giganteum* and *A. karataviense* for larger cutflowers, and *A. atropurpureum*, *A. neapolitanum* and *A. sphaerocephalon* for smaller cutflowers. Colchicums make lovely cutflowers, but note that colchicum sap is quite poisonous; while it's unlikely that any children or pets would sample the sap, it's good to exercise caution with these cutflowers just to be safe.

Anemone blanda and *Anemone nemorosa* have also been used as cutflowers, but they are very tiny and must be placed in miniature vases. They also don't last very long—a few days at most. Frankly, I'd just leave these species in the garden where they put on a much better show. Leaving the flowers on the plants also allows them to set seed and spread, providing an even better show in the next season. Muscari flowers make excellent short-stemmed cutflowers.

Q: When is the best time to cut bulb flowers for bouquets and arrangements?

Practical Advice: Most cutflowers are best cut in the morning or late evening, during the cooler part of the day. Never cut during the heat of the day. Many bulb flowers are best cut when about half of the florets are open. Here's the general method.

- Cut the stems as long as possible, leaving as many leaves on the plant to ensure there is enough foliage left to support corm or bulb development.

- Use a sharp knife to avoid damaging the stem by crushing it.

- Remove any leaves and place the stems in cold water as soon as possible. (I prefer to carry a pail of cold water with me.) Set the container in a cool, dark place such as the garage or basement for at least two or three hours before displaying the cutflowers in a vase. This cooling allows the flowers a chance to absorb as much water as possible and thus extends their life.

- Change the water in the vase daily, adding floral preservative each time the water is changed. Every time you change the water, recut flower stems by removing 1–2 cm of stem. Use a sharp knife (not scissors) to avoid crushing the stem tissue. Be sure to keep gladiola flower spikes vertical or they will bend.

Tips for Cutting Daffodils

Daffodils come into bloom before most annuals and are often the first cutflowers people harvest from their gardens. Here are a few tips for bringing them indoors successfully.

- Never cut daffodils with a knife; instead, twist the stalk near the base of the plant—simply snap and pull. If you cut the stem, you won't get the white, solid portion of the stem, which keeps the stem from curling. Snapped daffodils last longer in the vase.

- The sap that oozes from daffodil stems after they have been cut contains chemicals that have detrimental effects on other cutflowers if placed in the same vase. Something in that sap causes the other cutflowers to wilt; this is why you shouldn't put daffodils in the same vase with other cutflowers.

- If you want to mix daffodils with other flowers, condition the daffodils for 24 hours by soaking the stem ends in warm water, and then add them to the mixed vase. Do not re-cut the stems or you'll have to recondition the daffodils.

- Daffodils may cause skin welts on some people, so if you're allergic wear gloves when handling them.

Q: Can you give me any tips for using dahlias for cutflowers?

Practical Advice: When the first dahlia flowers of the season open, it's always nice to bring a few into the house. Dahlias will survive only about a week in the vase, but they look great while they last. Follow the general method above with these specific tips.

- Don't cut dahlias before they open fully. The flowers are not fully expanded until they have been open for three to six days. Unlike most cutflowers, fully opened dahlias last longer than those blooms that have only just begun to open. This advice is particularly true for the decorative, cactus and fully double types. Single types and semi-double varieties open more quickly.

- Leave the longest stem possible on the plant. (If you have disbudded and disbranched your flowers, long stems shouldn't be a problem. See pages 99–101.) Leave several sets of leaves on the growing stem to encourage the next set of blooms. Always cut just above a joint so that the cutflower stalk has an open end.

Q: I want to cut some of my tulips for cutflowers, but I am worried that if I remove too much foliage there won't be enough left to nourish the bulb for next year's flowers. Any advice?

Practical Advice: When you cut the flower stem, leave at least the lowest and the largest leaf on the plant. Grow cutflower tulips in a very sunny location to maximize the opportunity for photosynthesis. I recommend the vegetable garden. It's easy to tuck in a row or two, the flowers require very little attention and it usually doesn't matter that the sometimes-unsightly foliage is left to die there.

The Science Behind It: I recommend Darwin varieties for tulips you plan to leave undisturbed in a cutting bed for several years. Almost all of the Darwins are sterile and vigorous. If you're interested in some of the different hybrid tulips like Triumphs—single and double early varieties and lily-flowered kinds—treat them as annuals.

5

Troubleshooting

No matter how diligent we may be, sometimes bulbs
run into trouble. Planning ahead and carefully maintaining
bulbs will forestall most difficulties, but it's tough to prevent
every eventuality. When your bulbs run into problems,
the best thing to do is to carefully examine the symptoms,
the environment, and review your own actions prior to
the trouble. If you can correctly diagnose the problem, you're
much closer to finding the solution.

Flowering

Q: I had great blooms last year from my bulbs, but this year the showing was quite poor. What went wrong?

The Science Behind It: If your bulbs bloomed during one season but not the next, you could be facing one of several problems.

- You may have removed the foliage before it had completely died down, so the bulbs did not replenish.

- If the bulbs were planted in lean soil and you did not fertilize, the bulbs may be too small to flower this year.

- The bulbs have too much competition from other plants.

- The bulbs are in an area of the garden that stays wet or has poor drainage.

- The garden may be shadier now, due to the growth of surrounding trees and shrubs. In this case, move the bulbs to a full-sun location. Remember, every garden has four dimensions: width, height, depth and time. A sunny spot in 2005 may be shady by 2010!

- The bulbs may be overcrowded and need dividing. To fix this problem, dig up the bulbs in late spring or early summer, after the foliage has almost, but not completely, died down. Separate the small bulbils from the main bulb and then replant them with more space between bulbs. Discard any old or dried-up bulbs. Be sure to water and fertilize the bulbs when they have finished blooming.

If your tulips don't bloom in subsequent years, there are a number of problems that might be the cause.

Jonquil narcissus 'Pipit' readily grows in mixed flower beds, rock gardens and containers.

- You moved or transplanted your bulbs. Some bulbs, certain varieties of daffodils for example, do not like transplanting and will take a year off from flowering until they adjust to their new environment. They may also bloom in the first year after you purchased them, but then be unable to produce a flower bud for the following year. Remember, the flower that is produced in the first spring had already developed the previous year under the watchful eye of a professional grower.

- The variety you have planted may not naturalize readily. Eventually, the bulbs will stop producing good flowers.

- Some hybrid varieties burn out after the first growing season—they don't flower well in subsequent seasons.

- The weather during the previous season may have been unusually severe and impaired the production of the embryonic flower.

- If you live in a climate with a hot summer, some bulbs (tulips) do very poorly in seasons after the first planting. This is because it is the long, cool season that allows nutrients to move to the bulb for good bulb formation. Excessive heat prevents good bulbs from forming. (In North America, the best bulb-producing regions are in the cooler parts of the northwestern USA and in southwestern Canada.)

I prefer to think of some hybrid bulbs as annuals. I plant them in the fall, enjoy their beauty in the spring, and dig them up when they're finished. That way I don't have to put up with the dying foliage.

67

Trumpet narcissus 'Mount Hood'

Q: My daffodils didn't bloom this year after several years of great flowers. What happened?

Practical Advice: There are several possible causes when daffodils fail to bloom. Check the long list of possibilities on the previous pages and the two below.

- Typically daffodil bulbs grown in a very small space or crowded too closely together suffer "blindness," a failure to produce blooms. Dig up the bulbs after the foliage has yellowed and then divide them, replanting them so that they are about twice the height of the bulb apart (usually about 10–15 cm, depending on the size of the bulbs). You can replant them immediately after lifting them, or you can store them in a cool, dry location with good air circulation and then replant them in the fall.

- The bulbs may have a virus, perhaps spread by insects such as aphids or thrips. Daffodils are susceptible to many viruses. The two most common are yellow stripe and mosaic virus. Yellow stripe manifests as fine streaks of yellow running along the length of the leaves. It tends to appear as the leaves emerge. By the second season, the plant is severely weakened. Mosaic symptoms include white blotches on the flowers, where the petals lose colour. Plant vigour, however, seems unaffected by this virus. In time however, infected bulbs lose their vigour and produce smaller, weaker growth; eventually, they may stop blooming altogether. Viral infections are incurable. These bulbs should be dug up and destroyed—don't put them in your compost pile.

Q: The new bulbs I plant seem to bloom more than two weeks after my established bulbs. It extends the flowering season but it sure looks weird! Why the difference?

Practical Advice: That's always a bit of a surprise, isn't it? Assuming both groups of bulbs are planted in the same spot, it is common for newly planted bulbs to bloom a week or two earlier or later than the same variety already established in the garden. Blooming times vary because the flowers you see in the spring were set the previous summer in the climate where the bulbs were grown, which was likely different than yours. Don't worry. Next season's flowers will be initiated in your local growing environment, and next spring the newly planted bulbs will produce flowers at the same time as the older, established ones.

The Science Behind It: Sometimes bulbs will actually flower in the first year of planting two to three weeks earlier than the second year. In the case of fall-flowering colchicums, the flowers you see in the fall are set when the leaves die back in late spring or early summer. The bulbs are harvested by the grower and sold for late summer/early fall planting. The flowers emerge about ten weeks after the foliage dies. These bulbs are produced in a zone with an earlier spring than the zone where you may live; the flowers, therefore, emerge earlier the first year. In the second year, the flowering time is set by conditions in your area. You can expect the bloom-time to reflect your local conditions.

It is common for newly planted bulbs to bloom a week or two earlier or later than the same variety already established in the garden.

Q: I planted the same variety of bulbs in two different areas of the garden and they bloomed at different times. Why?

Practical Advice: The flowering time of bulbs can vary according to the microclimates in your garden. Bulbs planted in warmer, sunnier, more sheltered areas of the garden may bloom as much as two weeks earlier than those planted in shadier, cooler, more exposed locations.

The Science Behind It: Flowering times also vary according to seasonal variations from year to year and your geographical location. In areas with mild climates flowering can begin as early as late January, even though the main flowering period for that bulb is late February to early March. On the prairies, where the winters are longer, early bulbs typically begin blooming in early April.

Bulbs planted in warmer, sunnier, more sheltered areas of the garden may bloom as much as two weeks earlier than those planted in shadier, cooler, more exposed locations.

Some of the taller varieties of dahlia may require support—use attractive obelisks or easily camoflaged bamboo stakes.

Staking

Q: My dahlia snapped in a wind storm. Is there any hope for the plant? Should I stake my dahlias?

Practical Advice: That would depend on which part of the plant snapped and what time of year it happened. If sufficient branching has been left undamaged and it's early in the growing season, your dahlia may recover. If all of the stems have snapped but it's early in the season, the tuber may send up new growth but may not flower. If it is close to the end of the season and you have most of the plant, lift the tuber and store as you would normally. Some of the taller varieties may require support if they produce very large flowers or are growing in a windy, exposed location. Use green bamboo stakes: they are almost invisible in the garden. Another alternative is to plant taller varieties in a sheltered location, out of the wind and among shrubs, which will help support the plants as well as protect them

The Science Behind It: It is best to stake your dahlias at the time of planting. If you wait until later to set stakes in the ground, you risk damaging the tubers and root system. Tomato cages are great for this purpose; you can place the cages around the tubers right after you plant them. The plants grow through the centre of the rings, eliminating the need to tie up the plants. The metal cage quickly disappears from view as the foliage of the fast-growing dahlia engulfs it.

Suberization

Whenever a plant has been injured and its inner tissues exposed, a response is demanded. Plants react to wounds by producing suberin, a corky material that seals the wound and reduces the chance of water loss and infection.

A damaged begonia tuber that has produced suberin.

Q: We have a windy garden, and my gladiolus plants get knocked down. Should I stake them?

Practical Advice: Because of the way they grow, glads are not normally staked. However, giving the plants some extra anchorage may help. When you plant your glads, dig a trench 5–10 cm deeper than the recommended planting depth. Cover the corms with 5 cm of soil. When the shoots emerge, cover them with another 5 cm of soil and repeat the process until you reach soil level. When the shoots are about 20 cm above soil level, hill up soil around their bases.

If your garden is particularly windy, you may also want to plant the bulbs in a sheltered location—along a fence, for example. If you're growing them along a fence, you can try running a line of unobtrusive green garden twine from one end of the planting to the other. Tie the twine around a nail at either end, leave a little slack and your glads should be able withstand forceful winds.

Large-flowering gladiolus 'Wine & Roses'

By the end of the growing season, healthy gladiolus corms will have developed tiny cormels.

Pests

Q: I started some glad corms indoors and they were doing great. After about a week of hardening off, I transplanted them into the garden and they seemed to stall. Now they're short, with speckled brown edges, and there are no flowers in sight. What happened?

Practical Advice: It sounds like you've got some thrips. To identify these pests, tap the affected foliage or bloom over a piece of white paper. If you see tiny, slender, fast-moving black insects, they are thrips. Treat the plants with malathion. These common pests of gladioli often overwinter on the corms; that's why it's always a good idea to treat the corms before you plant them by simply soaking the corms for three hours in a solution of Lysol before planting. Of course, this won't eliminate the thrips that come from other plants during the summer.

The Science Behind It: There are many species of thrips, and as many targets for their voracious appetites. These tiny, slender insects multiply rapidly in hot, dry weather and cause stippling of leaves and flowers. Thrips are difficult to control because they are thigmotactic—they like to squeeze into the tiny places between petals and leaves, which makes chemical control difficult. Not all thrip species are bad; some like to dine on other thrips and other insect pests.

Bulb beds at the Butchart Gardens in Victoria, British Columbia, are protected from animal damage by covering the beds with large nets.

Squirrel damage on a hyacinth.

Q: I am having a problem with rodents eating my bulbs. Can I use some type of barrier to stop them?

Practical Advice: My first suggestion, and I hope it doesn't appear flip, is to simply plant bulbs that are not attractive to rodents (see page 77). A variety of rodents love bulbs and each has its own way of getting to them. Tailor the barrier to the pest and the bulbs. Here are some other suggestions.

• If animals are digging up your newly planted bulbs from the surface, try covering the planting area with plastic netting. Netting is easy to find at your local garden centre; it's cheap and easily cut. It is also dully coloured and virtually disappears once it's laid on the ground. You can also use wire mesh or window screens. Leave the barrier in place for at least two weeks to allow the soil to settle and the scent of the bulbs to diminish (rodents are attracted by both the scent and the loose soil).

- Another suggestion is to plant your bulbs a little deeper than normal and tamp the soil down firmly to make it more difficult for animals to dig. Rodents tend to be attracted to loose, freshly dug soil. After the soil has been firmly packed, water it well and mulch it immediately with about 5 centimetres of chopped leaves or bark mulch.

- If burrowing rodents are attacking your bulbs, try lining the transplanting hole with window screen or fine wire mesh before setting the bulbs into the ground. You can also buy plastic liners from a garden centre in the fall. These shallow, wide-mouthed baskets are set into the ground and then the bulbs are set inside them. For complete protection from mice and voles, you can also set chicken wire over the top of the baskets. Don't use window screen or any type of wire mesh that has smaller holes than chicken wire because the new shoots won't be able to grow up through the barrier. Mixing a bit of sharp crushed gravel or shells among the newly transplanted bulbs may also act as a deterrent to rodents.

A number of mammals, such as squirrels (top right) and rabbits (above) love to eat the tender new growth of bulbs. The best defence is to plant varieties that they find unpalatable.

75

Fritillaria imperialis *'Crown Imperial'* *is rarely bothered by mammal pests.*

- If animals are eating the top growth of the bulbs in the spring, rather than the bulbs themselves, you can cover the area with chicken wire or netting for a few weeks. Some gardeners say that sprinkling the planting area with blood meal acts as a deterrent. You can also spray the area with a product called Ro-pel. It is a bitter, non-toxic repellent that deters animals, but it must be reapplied after rain.

- Controlling grubs in your garden may also help because grubs are a favourite of gophers. If you remove their food source, the gophers may go elsewhere, which in turn will help eliminate problems caused by voles. Voles use gopher tunnels to move through the ground and also love to eat bulbs. You can also put a handful of sharp gravel around each newly planted bulb to discourage burrowing pests.

Rodents are most commonly a problem with new plantings. Once bulbs are well established, animals don't usually bother them.

Q: Which bulbs are rodent resistant?

Practical Advice: Narcissus are the most rodent resistant of all the bulbs, but there are also other bulbs that rodents dislike. These include *Allium* spp., *Crocus tommasinianus*, *Eranthis* spp., *Fritillaria imperialis*, *Galanthus* spp., *Hyacinthoides hispanica*, *Leucojum* spp., *Muscari* spp., *Scilla* spp. and *Ornithogalum nutans*.

Ornithogalum nutans is one bulb that rodents strongly dislike.

Bulbs On the Move

Perennial bulbs may work up, that is push up out of the ground for a number of reasons. This is a problem because bulbs near the soil surface are susceptible to drying out, cold temperatures and attack by rodents. Soil erosion from heavy rains or heaving from frost can cause bulbs to pop out of the ground. Mulching in the fall, after the ground has frozen, with a 5 to 10 cm layer of bark mulch, may help alleviate this problem if heavy spring rains are a regular occurrence in your area.

Overcrowding can also cause emergence, which is more often a problem with smaller bulbs because they are planted fairly shallowly. Corms that form new corms on top of the old one, dry and wither. During this process the corm produces long, fleshy contractile roots that normally pull the corms, both old and new, deeper into the ground. However, if the soil is very dry or hard, or if the corm is very close to the surface, this root may end up pushing the corm up and out of the ground—exactly the opposite of nature's intention. Dividing overcrowded bulbs will help alleviate this problem.

Poisonous Bulbs

Q: Which bulbs are poisonous? I have small children and I'm concerned that one of them might eat some of my bulbs.

Practical Advice: There are actually very few recorded cases of children being poisoned by plants; I searched both the Canadian and American poison control centre websites and was unable to find even one case of a child poisoned by the consumption of a flower bulb. But that doesn't mean that you shouldn't be vigilant. And note that sometimes it's not the bulb but the other parts of the plant that are harmful. Most of the cases of recorded plant poisonings are classed as "suspected" poisonings, usually after a child eats or touches a plant the parents believe to be poisonous. In the bulk of these cases, the "poisoning" turns out to be nothing more than common dermatitis.

That said, colchicum and gloriosa lily are extremely poisonous, even if consumed in small quantities. *Arisaema* and *Arum* are poisonous. *Amaryllis, Galanthus, Iris, Narcissus, Ornithogalum* and *Scilla* are somewhat harmful if eaten. *Alstromeria, Arum, Hyacinthus, Iris, Narcissus, Ornithogalum, Scilla* and *Tulipa* may also cause skin irritation if handled without gloves.

All parts of colchicum are considered poisonous.

6

Species & Varieties

General advice can come in handy for a wide range of gardening problems, but sometimes you need more specific tips. That's especially true of bulbs, which come in a myriad of species and varieties, each with its own strengths, weaknesses and care requirements. Whether you're growing alliums or tulips—or anything in between—it pays to know each bulb's ins and outs.

Allium giganteum

Alliums ❧ *Allium* spp.

Q: Which species of alliums are the easiest to grow?

Practical Advice: *Allium aflatunense, A. cernuum, A. moly, A. oreophilum* and *A. sphaerocephalon* are easy to grow, inexpensive and very reliable. *A. cernuum* is also the hardiest allium species.

Q: How do alliums propagate?

Practical Advice: After the flowers have dried and turned brown, you will notice that each floret opens to reveal shiny black seeds. Each seed will eventually fall to earth to produce a new allium plant. If you want to prevent alliums from spreading, simply remove the old flowerheads after they have finished flowering and before they set seed. Easy as pie!

The Science Behind It: Most, but not all, *Allium* species produce seed, and some do so more readily than others. Named cultivars—such as 'Firmament', 'Gladiator' and 'Ivory Queen'—normally don't produce seed; if they do, the quality is inferior and the plants may not grow true to type. *Allium* 'Globemaster' and *A. macleanii* (also known as *A. elatum*) do not produce seed. All alliums are true-bulbs and produce offsets.

Q: What causes the tips of allium leaves to become brown and dry even when the plants are well watered?

The Science Behind It: The life cycle of members of the allium family is very different from those of other flowering bulbs. Flowering occurs at the end of the growing cycle. This means that immediately after the bulbs have finished flowering they are ready to be harvested or, if you desire, moved. The foliage is of no further use to the bulb, so it begins to die, creating the brown foliage. Gardeners notice that browning is more of a problem for *A. giganteum*, but that's because the leaves of this species are so large that browning is particularly noticeable. Browning is accelerated if conditions are very dry or the humidity is very low.

Q: My alliums have developed orange pustules on the leaves. What is the problem and what can I do to fix it?

The Science Behind It: The problem you are seeing is a fungal disease called rust. Unfortunately, once you see the problem the only solution is to destroy the affected plants. Make sure that you remove all the leaves, flowers and bulb of the infected plant and destroy the plant material. Do not place it in your compost pile. Feed alliums with a fertilizer that is high in potassium; this can help prevent future occurrences.

Allium cernuum, *considered the hardiest allium species, readily produces seed.*

Allium karataviense

Allium aflatunense

Q: Can you suggest some plants I can interplant with alliums?

Practical Advice: Alliums look really pretty mixed with other purple-flowering perennials such as heather, iris, pyrethrum, lavender, salvia and flowering sage. For a stunning contrast, mix them with yellow-flowering perennials such as perennial daisies, lilies, foxglove, sedum and solidago.

If you are growing large-leafed or tall varieties (such as *A. giganteum* or *A. aflatunense*), the perennials will help prevent the large flowerheads from falling over and will hide the dying foliage.

Q: What are the best species of alliums to grow in pots in my garden?

Practical Advice: To grow alliums in pots successfully you must live in an area with milder winters (generally Zone 5 or warmer). I would recommend *A. karataviense, A. christophii* and *A. unifolium* because they have particularly nice foliage and large flowerheads, and they're not too tall—important characteristics for container gardening.

Q: I want to remove the spent flowerheads from my alliums to use in dried arrangements. If I do this, will I cause problems for future flower production?

The Science Behind It: No, old flowerheads can be removed at any time. The part of the plant that is crucial to replenishing the bulb's energy is the foliage, not the flowers and stems.

If you leave the spent blooms on long enough for most of the seeds to be released (on those alliums that produce viable seed), you can have the best of both worlds: new plants from seed and flowers for your arrangements. The alliums that produce the most attractive flower heads for dried arrangements are *A. christophii, A. karataviense* and *A. sphaerocephalon.*

Anemones ✌ *Anemone* spp.

Q: I've heard that *Anemone coronaria* is a good choice for planting outdoors in containers. I'd like to try this. Is there any special method I should know about?

Practical Advice: *Anemone coronaria* should be planted in late winter or early spring. The key is to soak the tubers in water overnight before you plant them. Soaking will plump them up and give them a good, quick start, but don't delay planting the tubers or flowering will be diminished. Plant in high-quality potting soil. If possible, plant the tubers with the protruding

Anemone blanda *'White Splendour'*

Tuberous begonia 'Non-Stop Salmon'

knobs pointing upwards (you can't always tell, though, so give it your best guess). Plant them closer than you would if you were planting in the garden. (I like to plant mine about 8 cm deep and the same distance apart.) Water the container well and put it in a warm, sunny, somewhat sheltered location. Fertilize with 20-20-20.

If you're really ambitious, here's a little trick. Make successive plantings in pots every two weeks until mid to late June, and you will have a show of colour through till the fall. About the time the first pot has finished flowering, the second one should be ready to burst into bloom.

Tuberous Begonias
ᨠ *Begonia* x *tuberhybrida*

Q: I would like to try growing my begonias from seed. Can I try this at home?

Practical Advice: Yes, but the tubers will be extremely small and difficult to carry over to the following growing season. Growing tuberous begonias from seed is much more difficult than starting them from tubers. For starters, the seed is extremely tiny, like dust, and very expensive—a gram of begonia seed is worth far more than a gram of gold! (You do get your money's worth though: one gram of begonia seed would give you hundreds of thousands of plants.) And even if you can afford the seed, growing it is a slow, painstaking process that requires patience and special care. 'Non-stop', 'Ornament', 'Pin-Up', 'Illumination', 'Panorama' and 'Clips' are some of the tuberous begonia series that are now available from seed. They will generally grow true to type.

Q: I purchased begonia tubers this past spring. The package said the flowers would be double. Most of them are, but my plants are also producing some single flowers. Why?

The Science Behind It: The smallest of the single flowers are the female (pistillate) flowers. Begonias require both male and female flowers in order to reproduce. These female blooms are not very showy and can be pinched off if you don't like them. The largest and showiest of the single flowers and all of the big double blooms are the male (staminate) flowers.

Q: If I can't store the tubers from my 'Nonstop' begonia plants, can I bring them in as houseplants to get me through the winter months?

Practical Advice: When bringing your plants indoors, be careful not to invite some very unwelcome guests inadvertently. Minor outdoor pests can often become a serious problem indoors because the typical home provides a near-perfect environment for insects. The warm temperatures are ideal for insect growth and reproduction, and houses lack predators like birds,

Tuberous begonia 'Non-Stop Yellow'

ladybugs and lacewings that keep pest populations down. There's no rain indoors to wash pests off plant foliage. Finally, there are no cold snaps indoors to snuff out bugs—unless your furnace goes on the fritz, and if that happens at -30°C, you've got bigger problems than bugs! Pests may also infest your existing houseplants.

To reduce the risk of this kind of calamity, isolate any plants you bring indoors for at least a few weeks until you can determine whether you've brought any insects indoors.

The Science Behind It: If wishes were horses, begonias would reside indoors as houseplants…but wishes aren't horses. Many people think that because tuberous begonias thrive outdoors in shady conditions they will grow easily in the house. This is not true, mainly because of the difference in light levels indoors and outdoors. Light levels inside the house, especially during the winter months, are very low. Even on a cloudy day plants in the garden will receive at least twice as much light as indoor plants growing in a bright, south-facing window. In such low light, plants produce only soft, weak growth, and often die. And in any event, the short days of winter cause dormancy in begonias. To grow begonias indoors successfully, you will require supplementary grow lights.

Tuberous begonia 'Non-Stop Rose Petticoat'

Zantedeschia *'Black Magic'* and *'Majestic Red'*

Calla Lilies ∾ *Zantedeschia* spp.

Q: My calla lily bulbs were growing well in an indoor container. Now the stems are weak and soggy, and some have started to fall off at soil level. What's wrong?

Practical Advice: When callas are first potted up, they prefer a soil temperature of 18–21°C until the new shoots have emerged fully. After leaves have begun to unfurl, the soil temperature should be reduced to 15–17°C. An environment that is too warm and wet will promote weak, soft growth that is vulnerable to disease. These conditions are perfect for the development of soft rot and other diseases.

The Science Behind It: Soft rot is caused by the bacterium *Erwinia caratovora*. The bacteria is carried on the bulbs and can easily destroy the bulbs once it gets going. Part of the reason for this susceptibility is that the optimal growing conditions for calla lilies (moist and very warm) are also the optimal growing conditions for *Erwinia*; once the plants are in a weakened state, the bacterium infects them readily. *Erwinia*-infested bulbs have an awful smell that is unique.

Q: I have had problems with soft rot in my calla rhizomes. Any suggestions to help control this in the future?

Practical Advice: I'm not afraid to resort to clichés when they're accurate, so here is one: an ounce of prevention is worth a pound of cure. In other words, the best control method for soft rot is prevention. Try to choose firm, blemish-free rhizomes, provide optimum growing conditions and keep your plants as healthy and vigorous as possible.

The Science Behind It: Soft rot is caused by *Erwinia* bacteria. And while the majority of calla lily rhizomes are commercially produced by tissue culture, and tissue culture eliminates *Erwinia*, the unfortunate truth is that these tissue-cultured bulbs are planted in the ground where they can pick up the disease. Still, tissue-cultured bulbs are a better hedge against soft rot than callas propagated by other means.

Q: I grew some calla lilies as annuals in my garden this year. They bloomed for a while and now they have finished. Will they flower again?

Practical Advice: Not this year. Calla lilies grow from rhizomes. Depending upon the size of the rhizome, each one will produce anywhere from one to five blooms—but only once per season.

Once they open, calla flowers should last three to four weeks. If it is really hot and dry, the blooming season will be shortened. Fortunately, the foliage is also very attractive, so the plants make a striking contribution to the garden even after the flowers are finished.

The Science Behind It: After flowering is complete, the rhizome continues to produce leaves. It also increases in size, storing resources for the next growing season. Once the temperature begins to cool off in the fall, the plant will go dormant. You can keep your callas from year to year by digging up the rhizomes before the first fall frost and storing them in a cool, dark indoor location.

Zantedeschia 'Crystal Blush'

Canna *'Pink Princess'*
(above); Canna *'Pretoria'*
(Bengal Tiger) (left)

Canna Lilies ❧ *Canna* spp.

Q: When I go to the garden centre to choose canna lilies, I feel overwhelmed and am not sure which variety to choose. Can you help?

Practical Advice: The best way to choose your cannas is to decide what you would like the final size of your plant to be, where you are going to plant it and how you are going to use it in your garden. Check the packages for final heights from the suitable varieties. Cannas are not formally classified and are typically grouped as short (less than 1 m), medium (2–3 m) and tall varieties (over 2 m). After you've figured out the most desirable height, decide which flower and foliage colour you like.

Q: I started my canna bulbs inside my house and then transplanted them outdoors about a week ago. There have been no night frosts, but the leaves look scorched. I know canna lilies like lots of sun, so that can't be the problem. What's wrong?

Practical Advice: The night temperatures in your area are probably still dropping to fairly low levels at night. Although it hasn't frozen, cool temperatures or cool winds have caused injury, giving the leaves a scorched appearance. Cannas do not tolerate temperatures in the low single digits, especially after they have been growing indoors. That being said, the dam-

Canna 'Phasion'

age is superficial and the cannas will recover once temperatures warm up. Try placing a few bamboo stakes in the soil around the cannas. With this support, you can throw a blanket or sheet over the plants at night until the weather has warmed up.

The Science Behind It: Note that if you grow your bulbs in the home and then place them straight outside, the leaves can't adapt quickly enough to the intense sunlight. It's better to give your cannas a gradual transition to the great outdoors.

Q: I want to store my cannas over the winter, but I'm concerned I won't be able to remember which variety is which. Any suggestions?

Practical Advice: I like to label each canna before I lift it. Using a permanent marker, write the variety name on a plastic or metal tag with a hole in it, or even on the rhizome itself if it's large enough. When you lift the rhizome, leave about 15 cm of the stem attached and tie the label to the rhizome with string or thin wire. Tie it tightly because the stems will shrivel during storage and you don't want the label to fall off. If you have several rhizomes of the same cultivar, store each type in a box and label the outside of the box.

Q: I have a small conservatory attached to my house. Can I grow my cannas in pots in the greenhouse year-round?

Practical Advice: Go ahead! Cannas can be grown year-round in a greenhouse. All cultivars will grow in this situation, but of course some grow better than others.

The Science Behind It: Cannas grown indoors require year-round temperatures of at least 10°C for growth and flowering to continue during the winter months. The containers must have good drainage. Use a high quality soilless mixture in the pots and be sure you keep the plants well watered. If they are very large and it is really hot, they may require watering twice a day. Cannas can stand a small amount standing water, but only when they are growing actively. In the spring and fall, during periods of less active growth and before the root system is well established, don't allow them to stand in water. If cannas become rootbound in the container, they will begin to decline in both vigour and flower production. At this point, they require division and separation.

Q: What are water cannas?

The Science Behind It: Water cannas are less well known than and not as widely available as *C. indica* hybrids, although the two species are closely related. Water cannas are hybrid cultivars derived from *C. glauca* and crossed with other hybrids. They were first developed by Robert Armstrong in the l970s. They tend to have a willowy growth habit and look very graceful. Unlike most cannas, which require full sun and rich, well-drained soil to grow successfully, water cannas can be grown as a marginal aquatic beside ponds or as bog plants in plastic baskets around the edge of a garden pool. They will survive with up to 15 cm of water above the rhizome. Water cannas require full sun and grow best in areas with hot summers; they prefer pools that warm up quickly. In areas with cold winters, they must be lifted and stored like other cannas, but in milder climates (Zone 7 and above) they will survive outdoors as a perennial.

The best-known water canna cultivars are 'Endeavour', 'Erebus', 'Ra' and 'Taney'.

Canna *'Apricot Dream'*

91

Chionodoxa luciliae

Chionodoxa ☙ *Chionodoxa* spp.

Q: I want to plant some chionodoxa bulbs in my garden, but I would also like some other little spring bulbs that would flower about the same time. What do you suggest?

Practical Advice: Try *Eranthis hyemalis, Galanthus, Scilla siberica, Puschkinia scilloides, Tulipa kaufmanniana, T. tarda* and *T. turkestanica.* Chionodoxas also look beautiful planted among a number of spring-flowering perennials, such as aubretia, pulmonaria, hellebores, hepatica, primroses, pulsatilla and *Phlox douglasii.*

Q: Can you explain the difference between *Chionodoxas* and *Scillas*?

The Science Behind It: Austrian botanist Franz Speta originally decided that there were insufficient grounds to separate the genera *Chionodoxa* and *Scilla,* so he merged them, although he retained *Chionodoxa* as a subgenus of *Scilla.* Botanists have since reinstated *Chionodoxa* as a distinct genus. Both bulbs produce tiny, mostly blue, star-shaped flowers on racemes early in the spring. Both also have white and pink cultivars. The biggest visible difference is the configuration of the stamens.

Once you know what to look for, distinguishing between *Chionodoxas* and *Scillas* is easy. In *Chionodoxa*, the six petals of the flower surround six stamens that have flattened filaments arranged close together, giving them the appearance of a central white cone. In *Scilla*, the stamens have thread-like filaments. This central feature distinguishes *Chionodoxas* from *Scillas*. *Chionodoxas* also produce a single pair of strap-like leaves, while *Scillas* can produce up to 15 leaves.

Some chionodoxas hybridize naturally with *S. bifolia*; for instance, a naturally occurring hybrid of *C. forbesii* pollinates with *S. bifolia* to produce a little bulb known as *Chionoscilla allenii*. But most scillas are not closely related to chionodoxas.

Colchicums ⚭ *Colchicum* spp.

Q: What is colchicum?

Practical Advice: Colchicum is a fall-flowering bulb, hardy to Zone 4 (Zone 3 with winter protection). It is sometimes confused with autumn-flowering crocus because it is purchased and planted in late summer or early fall and flowers a few weeks later. It may even be referred to as giant autumn-flowering crocus, but this is a misnomer. Colchicum flowers have six stamens, while crocus flowers have only three.

Colchicum *'Lilac Wonder'*

Colchicum autumnale

The flowers appear in the fall, without leaves. The leaves appear in late winter or spring and last until early summer. Colchicum leaves are large and may interfere with other plants in the spring, so I prefer to plant clumps of colchicum on their own rather than mix them with other plants. Colchicums prefer partially shady locations and are ideal planted under deciduous trees or among shady perennials. The late-flowering varieties, which flower after the trees have dropped their leaves, are especially gorgeous because the fallen leaves not only set off the brightly coloured flowers, but also support them as they emerge and lengthen (pictured on page 52). The leaves also help hide the lighter-coloured, tube-shaped flower stems. Colchicums are great for late-season colour.

Q: I've heard colchicums called dry-flowering bulbs. What does that mean?

Practical Advice: A dry-flowering bulb is one that will flower without being planted in soil—or in any medium at all. They can be placed on a windowsill in a saucer and bloom—they don't even require moisture. After flowering, the corms can be planted in the garden and will grow successfully. Remember, though, that once the corms have bloomed inside the house they won't rebloom in the garden until the following fall.

The Science Behind It: All colchicums are considered dry-flowering, but some species are definitely better than others for this purpose. C. byzantium 'The Giant' is the best dry-flowering colchicum. The white cultivars and double-flowering cultivars do not grow well as dry-flowering bulbs.

Q: What is tessellation?

Practical Advice: Tessellation is checkered patterning; many colchicums feature subtle tessellation on their petals. Tessellated varieties typically flower later than other colchicums, in late autumn and early winter. They tend to produce larger flowers and are more susceptible to being spoiled by inclement weather. Two species that have tessellated petals are *C. agrippinum* and *C. bivonae*. Both can be difficult to obtain but are well worth the effort if you can find them.

Q: I know that I'm not supposed to cut back the leaves of my colchicum bulbs. Can I remove the spent flowers?

The Science Behind It: Spent flowers may indeed be cut off, or you can leave them on the plant to fall on their own; neither action will affect the corm's life cycle. Some gardeners prefer to remove the dying flowers because they look a bit messy, particularly on cultivars that produce a succession of blooms over a period of weeks. Dead foliage can also be tidied up and removed in the early summer, but not until it has died back fully.

Crocuses ✍ *Crocus* spp.

Q: Can I plant a groundcover over my crocuses?

Practical Advice: Sure, as long as you use low-growing groundcovers that are not too dense. Try *Phlox subulata, Arenaria, Dianthus* spp. and *Vinca minor*.

Q: I would like to plant crocuses with some early-flowering perennial plants in my flowerbeds. What do you suggest?

Practical Advice: Choose smaller, early-flowering perennial plants such as aubretia, pulmonaria, hellebores, hepatica, primroses, pulsatilla and *Phlox douglasii*.

Q: I think I'm unusual because I prefer fall-flowering crocuses. Can you recommend any perennials that will show them off nicely?

Practical Advice: It's not unusual to love fall-flowering crocuses! The bronze or deep-burgundy leaves of ajugas contrast beautifully with *C. speciosus*. Other black-leafed, low-growing perennials are also stunning, such as *Geranium* 'Hocus Pocus' and heuchera.

Q: Are bees attracted to crocus flowers?

Practical Advice: Bees like crocuses even more than the typical gardener does! Because crocuses typically bloom before many other plants, it is quite common to see bees collecting food from crocus flowers. Bees feed on the pollen, which provides some of their first food after the long winter months. Some bee species will feed as soon as daytime temperatures rise above 11 or 12°C.

Q: Is it true that the spice saffron comes from crocus flowers?

The Science Behind It: It sure does; if you're just mad about saffron, you should really love crocuses. In ancient times, saffron was obtained by drying the bright-orange stigmas of the autumn-flowering *Crocus sativus* over a fire. It was considered an invaluable medicine in ancient Egypt. Saffron has also been used as a dye.

Today, 80 percent of the saffron produced comes from Spain. It is field grown and typically harvested during the month of November. The bright-orange stigmas are plucked from each flower by hand and quickly dried. Saffron is one of the world's most expensive spices, commanding prices of hundreds of dollars per ounce. The stigmas of 150,000 crocus flowers are needed to produce a kilogram of saffron! Saffron is used in gourmet cooking for its colour, scent and flavour.

Crocus biflorus *'Miss Vain'*

Crocus chrysanthus *'Goldilocks'*

Q: Are prairie crocuses bulbs? Can I dig some up and put them in my garden?

The Science Behind It: Once again, a plant's common name obscures its true nature. The plants commonly referred to as prairie crocuses are not in fact bulbs nor for that matter, even crocuses. *Pulsatilla vulgaris*, often called pasqueflower, is seen blooming on the prairie in early spring. The plants have soft, ferny foliage and lovely blooms that develop into fluffy seed heads. The name "prairie crocus" refers to the shape of the bloom, and to the fact that they flower quite early. Rather than dig these beauties up from their natural habitat, purchase them from your local garden centre where they are available both as seeds and as potted plants. These plants are not taken from the wild, but are propagated by commercial growers.

Dahlias ⁊ *Dahlia rosea*

Q: What is pruning as it applies to dahlias?

Practical Advice: In the greenhouses, we prune dahlias so that they will produce more branches, and thus more flowers. Pruning dahlias involves removing the tips of the main stem once three or four sets of leaves have developed. This helps to develop a lower-growing, more floriferous and

97

often self-supporting plant—that is, a plant that doesn't require staking. When you prune dahlias, remember that you are encouraging your plants to bush out more fully; take this fact into account when you are determining how far to set them apart in the garden. Pruned plants will require more space than unpruned plants of the same variety.

The Science Behind It: You should definitely prune your dahlias. When dahlias are left unpruned, they tend to stretch like a bean pole that bears flowers only at the top and is susceptible to breakage in the wind. If you're growing dahlia flowers for exhibition, pruning takes on an entirely different meaning, but that's a topic for another discussion.

Q: How do I prune my dahlias?

Practical Advice: During the first month of growth, dahlias should be pinched by removing the tip of each new plant shoot. Pinch tall varieties once they have developed four leaves, small varieties when the shoots have six leaves. Growth is diverted to the shoots in the leaf axils, and the pay-off is a bushier, stockier, better-flowering plant. Keep pruning until the dahlias are 40–45 cm tall. For best flower and form, tall varieties should be kept to four to six stems, medium varieties eight to ten stems, and smaller varieties to ten to twelve stems.

Decorative dahlia 'Cafe Au Lait'

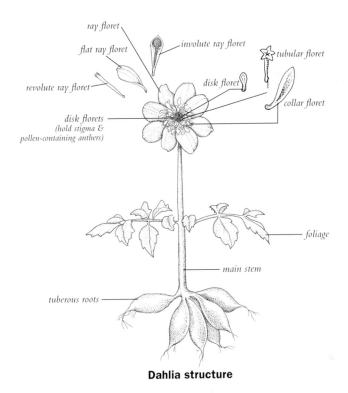

ray floret

flat ray floret

involute ray floret

tubular floret

revolute ray floret

disk floret

collar floret

disk florets
(hold stigma &
pollen-containing anthers)

foliage

main stem

tuberous roots

Dahlia structure

Q: What is disbranching?

Practical Advice: Disbranching, also known as "pinching," is the act of removing a plant's side shoots or branches. Smaller shoots can be simply rubbed out with your thumb as they begin to develop, and larger branches can be cut out. This procedure can be used if your dahlia plants have been left to grow without pinching and have become a tangle of weak growth. If this crowded growth is left unattended, the tissue may harden and the dahlia may produce fewer, smaller blooms. Disbranching opens up the plant habit, provides more light and space to the remaining stems and branches, and encourages stronger growth.

The Science Behind It: There are three main methods of disbranching. The first is single-stem branching. This method is typically used by people growing flowers for exhibitions, and it produces plants that are not particularly attractive but bear stunning, extra-large flowers. Allow the plant to grow until the first cluster of flower buds forms at the end of the stem. Then remove the two side buds, leaving the centre flower bud (disbudding—see the following question). Remove the small shoots that are beginning to develop in the leaf axils for several leaf sets below the top of the

99

Gallery dahlia 'Art Deco'

stem (disbranching). The result is a single strong stem with a large showy flower. Once this flower is removed or cut, allow one of the lower shoots to grow and repeat the procedure when the flower buds form. The plant will require staking.

The second method of disbranching is called multiple stem branching. This method produces stocky, low-growing plants that have a full, bushy habit. It also produces lots of good-sized showy flowers. Pinch out the top shoots of the plant as soon as three or four sets of leaves have developed on each stem. Plants pinched this way produce very sturdy growth that doesn't usually need staking. I find the absence of stakes and the overall look of the plant very attractive in garden or landscape plantings.

The third method of disbranching is called the combination system. The first flower bud is allowed to develop and then all the side shoots below it are removed, except for the two or three pairs closest to the ground. These are allowed to develop flower shoots.

If all these methods sound complicated, don't be intimidated. Once you've pinched a few of your own dahlias, the job will become second nature.

Q: What is disbudding?

Practical Advice: Disbudding, also known as "debudding," means removing some of a plant's flower buds; it is usually done with dahlias. Disbudding serves two purposes: to control flower size and to modify the timing of the blooms. The procedure is typically used by gardeners who are growing their dahlias for flower shows; they need large, spectacular flowers for certain dates.

This is not an attractive look in the garden, even though the resulting flower will be spectacular. Most people prefer just to prune their dahlias and avoid disbudding altogether. But disbudding can play an important role for the home gardener growing larger-flowered varieties. It ensures that you get great big flowers for show and for cutting.

Q: My dahlias are stunted and growing very poorly. What is the problem?

The Science Behind It: Stunting is one of the most baffling dahlia problems. The term is used loosely to describe plants exhibiting hardened stem tissues and poor, undersized growth. Stunting is the plant's response to stress, although the stressor can be difficult to identify.

There isn't much you can do for a stunted dahlia, but here is a method to try. Cut back the main stems just above the new shoots at the base of the plant. (If all the stems are larger than this, cut the plant off about 6–8 cm above the lowest branches.) Give the plant plenty of water and keep it consistently moist—don't let it dry out. (Some people like to

Semi-cactus dahlia 'Harlequin'

create a large basin around dahlias. Filling this basin each time you water provides the plants with many litres of water that will slowly sink down to the roots.) Give the plant lots of fertilizer—try a good dose of 20-20-20 once a week. Lightly cultivate the soil around the plant to make sure it is loose and well aerated. Don't dig too deeply: you don't want to damage the plant's roots.

If the poor, undersized growth looks abnormal, there may another problem. Insects such as aphids or leaf hoppers may be the cause. There is also a virus called dahlia mosaic virus or true stunt. Characteristics of this virus include mosaic mottling of the leaves, yellowish stripes along the leaf veins, curled or distorted foliage, and small, underdeveloped stems and roots. As is the case with all viral infections, there is no cure. You must destroy all infected plants and roots. Do not put the plant material in your compost pile. It is important to remove infected plants because viruses can be transmitted by sucking insects such as aphids and thrips. Any cuttings taken from viral plants will also be infected.

Q: What is a dinnerplate dahlia?

Practical Advice: This is an unofficial category of dahlias that have been grouped together because of their extra-large flowers—roughly the size of dinner plates. They have been extremely popular with gardeners, so

Decorative dahlia 'Mistery Day'   *Dinnerplate dahlia 'Lavender Perfection'*

Dinnerplate dahlia 'Kelvin Floodlight'

breeders have been busily producing new varieties and colours. Most of the dinnerplate varieties are actually subcategories of Division 4 (waterlily dahlias) and Division 5 (decorative dahlias).

The Science Behind It: They are absolutely gorgeous, but because their flowers are so huge they are susceptible to damage in windy and exposed locations. The breeders have done a great job producing a massive inflorescence (flower), but they didn't have as much luck with the peduncle (flower stalk): in the wind, dinnerplate dahlias can flap around like crazy. Choose a sheltered spot and stake the plants. The blooms are often so heavy that the supporting stems fall over from the weight.

Q: I heard someone refer to dark dahlias. What are they?

Practical Advice: Most dahlias have glossy green leaves, but a few varieties have bronze or burgundy leaves. These varieties are called *dark dahlias*.

103

Peony-flowering dahlia 'Bishop of Llandoff'

I especially like these varieties because the dark foliage sets off the brightly coloured flowers beautifully. Perhaps the best-known dark dahlia is 'Bishop of Llandoff'. It has beautiful scarlet flowers and burgundy foliage. Breeders are paying attention to the intense consumer interest in these types of dahlias, and more dark-leafed varieties have become available in the past few years.

Q: I notice there are dahlias in packs available as bedding plants, but they're smaller than the dahlias I know. Are they the same as the dahlia bulbs that I buy from the garden centre?

Practical Advice: These dahlias are started from seed and are actually a different species: *Dahlia pinnata*. They are often called seed dahlias or bedding dahlias and are typically sold with bedding plants. You can also buy them as seed. They reach 30–40 cm and tend to bloom earlier than tuberous-rooted dahlias. Seed dahlias form small tubers by the end of the growing season, but the tubers are generally too small to overwinter successfully. If the tubers are large enough lift and store them as you would regular dahlias (see page 45 for lifting instructions). Because the tubers are very small, they are more prone to desiccation and often do not store successfully. Seed dahlias tend to be pretty inexpensive, so you must decide whether the extra work is worthwhile. It won't be a great cost saver.

Q: I bought some plants called dahliettas at a greenhouse last spring. Are these dahlias?

Practical Advice: Yes. Dahliettas are vegetatively propagated varieties that rarely grow taller than 20 cm. They produce masses of brightly coloured, fully double flowers. They look great in containers and smaller gardens.

Q: The dahlia tubers I planted in the garden last season seemed perfectly healthy but they never grew at all. Why?

Practical Advice: One possibility is that slugs ate the tender new shoots just as they were emerging. Check for telltale signs of slugs, such as the silver slime trails they leave behind. To prevent further problems, remove any boards or rocks that slugs may be hiding under, or try a combination of bait and traps. A friend of mine once lured slugs in between two boards, one held above the other by rocks; once the slugs were in place, he callously kicked away the stones and squashed the slugs to jelly. Cruel, but effective!

The Science Behind It: Of course, the slugs may be innocent; there are other reasons tubers fail to produce dahlias. Perhaps there were no eyes on the tubers. Without eyes, or growing points, the tubers cannot produce top growth. Also, if tubers are soft and desiccated, rather than firm, they will not grow; always give your tubers a squeeze at the greenhouse before you buy!

*Dahlietta 'Lizzy' (left)
and 'Patricia' (above)*

Alocasia macrorrhiza

Elephant Ears ∽ *Alocasia* spp. & *Colocasia* spp.

Q: Are elephant ears (also known as taros) edible?

The Science Behind It: Yes, certain cultivars of *Colocasia esculenta* are edible. However, the tubers contain oxalates—chemicals that may cause skin irritation when the tuber is handled. These crystals also give the tubers an irritating, acrid taste unless they are thoroughly cooked. If improperly prepared, the tubers can cause burning and swelling of the lips, mouth, tongue and throat. Ornamental elephant ear is typically used as a food only in survival situations—this isn't something you want to try at your next backyard barbeque.

However, there are taro cultivars that have been developed for eating. These edible species are commonly known as table taro. They tend to have large, tender leaves and comparatively low acidity. The corms are used in various Hawaiian and Asian dishes; the leaves may be used to wrap food.

Q: Can I overwinter my elephant ears if I live in a cold zone?

Practical Advice: The short answer is yes. One of our staff members, an avid gardener and a big fan of this plant, grows her elephant ears in a large pot. At the end of the season (before any frosts), she cuts the leaves back to just above soil level, brings the entire pot into her garage and quits watering it. The remaining stems die back on their own and are easily removed. In the late winter, she brings the pot into a warmer location in her house and begins to water it. By the time the weather warms up, her plant is growing actively and is ready to go outside. Her biggest challenge so far has been that after a couple of years the plant outgrows each container and has to be planted into an even larger one; then the container becomes so large and heavy that the logistics of moving it become the challenge.

The Science Behind It: The trick is to turn the bulb dormant before temperatures get too cold. Dormancy is triggered by a lack of water. About a month before you want to dig up the tuber (i.e., about a month before the average first fall frost), cut off the water. The leaves will start to wither and die. When most of the foliage has faded—and before a killing frost—dig up the tubers. Place the tubers in a cool, dry location (a heated garage or basement is fine) and leave them until any remaining leaves dry up and fall off. (In areas with warmer falls, tubers can be dried in shade.) The tubers will soon look dry and shriveled. Clinging soil and roots will also dry up and fall off.

Store tubers by hanging them in well-ventilated sacks in a dry, cool place (about 10°C) until winter or early spring. Masses of tubers will hold moisture much better than individual tubers (especially the smaller ones, which have a greater tendency to desiccate), so I leave the clumps together until spring. To separate the clumps, simply twist individual tubers free. Transplant tubers into pots at least six weeks before you want to plant the tubers outside. The size of the tubers varies greatly with elephant ears, so I use this general rule: plant them at a depth two times the width of the tuber. If there are any stem remnants left on the tuber, I try to ensure they rise to just about the soil level. Elephant ears are slow to break dormancy, but they grow quickly once they awaken.

Colocasia esculenta

Q: We had an unseasonably early frost the other night and I left my elephant ears out in the garden unprotected. The leaves are looking very frozen and mushy. Will it come back or have I killed it?

Practical Advice: Despite their tropical origins, elephant ears are actually pretty resilient. Slight freezing temperatures will damage the leaves, but the trunks will eventually sprout new leaves if the temperatures haven't gone below about -3°C. If you live in a zone where the plant is considered an annual, cut it back, dig it up and dry the tuber. (If you live in a zone with normally warm autumns, you can dry the tubers in open shade.) Don't wash the tuber! The soil will dry and fall off on its own. Store the tuber and plant it again next spring.

In future, if there is a risk of frost and you feel it's too early to lift the tuber, protect the plant by carefully placing a tall stake in the pot and covering it with a blanket (if you have one big enough!).

Q: I want to grow my elephant ears in containers. Do you have any tips?

Practical Advice: The main thing to remember is that the container must be very large. Elephant ear does not grow well in a container smaller than 60 cm in diameter. It will often outgrow this container in less than a single season, especially if conditions are optimum. If the plant becomes root-bound, top growth slows or stops. The good news is that once the roots are given more room, the top growth takes off again.

The Science Behind It: Plant the tubers in top-quality potting mix to a depth equivalent to two times the width of the tuber. If some stem is attached, be sure the tip emerges above the soil surface. It is imperative to keep elephant ears well watered. They do not tolerate drying out during their active growing season; this will cause poor growth and initiate dormancy. Fertilize the plant every two to three weeks during the period of active growth.

One fairly common problem is that these plants are so huge that they become top-heavy, so choose a heavy container. Half barrels work well. If you pick a light container the plants may fall over in the wind. I like to mix extra compost into the potting mixture to help retain moisture, add weight to the pot and optimize the soil conditions.

Eranthis hyemalis

Winter Aconite ~ *Eranthis* spp.

Q: Someone told me that *Eranthis* bulbs are referred to as *little bulbs*. I was wondering what exactly this means. Does this term include any other bulbs?

Practical Advice: The group of so-called little bulbs is actually a subset of the hardy spring-flowering bulbs. This grouping has no scientific basis; it was developed as a convenient way to refer to a range of small hardy species. The group typically includes *Chionodoxa, Eranthis, Galanthus, Leucojum, Muscari, Puschkinia, Scilla,* species narcissus and species tulips. Species crocuses may also be included, but crocuses are more typically grouped by themselves.

Q: How do winter aconite bulbs reproduce?

The Science Behind It: Winter aconite reproduces slowly through both tubers and seeds. The exception is the hybrid *Eranthis tubergenii*, which is a crossing of the two most common species, *E. cilicica* and *E. hyemalis.* This hybrid is sterile and can be propagated only by division. All eranthis species naturalize—more quickly if the bulbs are located in optimal conditions—but *E. tubergenii* naturalizes more slowly than the other two species.

Fritillaries ❧ *Fritillaria* spp.

Q: I'd like to try growing a few fritillaries in my yard, but I'm not confident. I know you list the easier-to-grow species, but I was wondering whether some of these are easier and more reliable to grow than others?

Practical Advice: The easiest of the easy-to-grow fritillaries are *Fritillaria meleagris*, *F. michailovskyi* and *F. pontica*.

Q: I heard there is a fritillary that can grow with minimal attention and a plentiful supply of moisture in both spring and summer? Which species is it?

Practical Advice: All fritillaries will grow better with a little bit of help, but *Fritillaria meleagris* and *F. pontica* are relatively carefree. As a rule, these two can cope with plentiful spring moisture as long as the soil is well drained,

Fritillaria meleagris

and they are even content with some moisture during the dormant summer months as long as the soil dries out at least periodically. They prefer soil temperatures that are reasonably cool, rather than baking hot, at bulb level.

Q: Which fritillary species grow best in shady gardens?

Practical Advice: *F. imperialis* and *F. pontica* are your best bets for shady spots.

Q: What about fritillary species that prefer drier conditions in the garden?

Practical Advice: One of the easiest to grow in these conditions is *Fritillaria assyriaca*. It will thrive in a sloped flowerbed in full sun where the soil gets quite hot and dry. An open flowerbed in a fully sunny location where the plant mix is relatively stable is a good location for *F. persica*. The key here is to make sure that the soil is also well drained.

Both of these species are indigenous to dry regions of the Middle East, so they should be quite suited to the drier areas of your garden.

Q: I planted some *Fritillaria imperialis* in my garden last fall. This spring, they produced leaves and stems but no flowers. What's wrong?

The Science Behind It: We've had this problem here as well, and the cause can be a little difficult to pin down. Still, I can offer a few suggestions that may produce a greater rate of success and more reliable flowering.

• The large bulbs of *F. imperialis* have a small hole at the top of the bulb where the previous year's stem died away. This opening tends to catch water, and moisture may sit there during the summer resting period, rotting the bulbs and causing the flowers to fail. To help alleviate this problem, plant the bulb tilted slightly sideways. (Some people argue that the bulb will right itself within a season, so there is no advantage to tilting the bulb. Personally, I think it's worth a try because if the bulb does right itself you haven't lost anything; if it doesn't, there is a definite advantage.)

• Plant *F. imperialis* deep in the ground. I recommend a depth of 25–45 cm in coarse soil or well-draining loam.

• During the active growing period, mulch the soil around the plants and give them a generous shot of all-purpose fertilizer every two weeks up to the time when they begin to flower. The nourishment helps to ensure that the plant can replenish the bulb and produce flowers again the following year. Remember, those huge flowers demand a lot of energy from the bulb.

Fritillaria pontica

- Fritillary roots do not like to be disturbed once the bulbs are planted. The roots will not regrow if they are broken, so it is crucial not to damage them when you cultivate near the plant. Again, deep planting will help to minimize this problem. If you must move your bulbs, do so in midsummer after the top growth has completely died back. At this point, the roots are finished and the bulb has gone dormant until the fall.

This may sound like an awful lot of extra work, but the unusual, spectacular flowers of this species (pictured on page 76) is well worth the effort required to get fritillaries established in your garden.

Q: What is the best way to store fritillary bulbs?

Practical Advice: The short answer is that you probably shouldn't store these bulbs. The best place for fritillaries is always in the ground, even for those species that prefer dry conditions during the dormant summer months. They bruise fairly easily and are subject to serious deterioration when out of the ground.

The Science Behind It: If you must store your fritillary bulbs, dust them with fungicide and cover them in peat moss or a similar material that has a degree of moisture but is not too wet. The storage medium should be damp-dry rather than moist. Then get the bulbs back into the soil as quickly as possible.

Snowdrops ∼ *Galanthus* spp.

Q: A few years ago, I managed to locate some unusual cultivars of snowdrops. Now the clumps have grown and gotten larger, and I'm having a hard time distinguishing them. Can you help?

The Science Behind It: This is a common problem with named cultivars from this genus. *Galanthus* species have a tendency to be highly variable, and variability is enhanced when the plants self-seed. Cultivars rarely produce offspring that is true to type—that is, very few generate daughter plants identical to their parents. If you want to keep your named cultivars distinct, you must remove any seed capsules before they ripen and start to shed their seeds. The clumps will then multiply more slowly, through the production of daughter bulbs only. You can also stick to double-flowering cultivars, which do not produce seed.

Q: I would like to plant some snowdrops in containers. Is this possible and, if it is, is there anything special I should know?

Practical Advice: Snowdrops are becoming a bit more popular for container planting, but they do present a challenge when grown in pots. Remember that bulbs planted in containers will not withstand temperatures as cold as those they can tolerate if they are planted in the ground; so, if you live in a zone that is on the edge of hardiness for *Galanthus*, I wouldn't recommend planting them in containers.

Galanthus nivalis

The Science Behind It: For best results, spend a little extra time preparing before you plant. Be sure the container has drainage holes. Place a layer of coarse gravel across the bottom of the container. Then add a layer of high-quality potting soil. Next, add a layer of loam mixed with lots of compost. Set the bulbs in the pot, planting them slightly closer than you would if you were planting them in the garden, about 4–6 cm apart.

To ensure success in containers year after year, it's best to remove the clump of bulbs from the pot after they have finished blooming and to replant them in a shadier spot in the garden where they can remain fairly cool and receive adequate moisture. The bulbs are prone to drying out when they are left in the containers, and drying out will kill them.

If you buy packaged bulbs, make sure you purchase and plant them as early as possible in the growing season. *Galanthus* bulbs are quite susceptible to drying out. To me, the best way to enjoy snowdrops in containers is to plant them green. *Green* means that you remove the snowdrops from the garden in the spring after the leaves have emerged, but before the flowers have opened. Some greenhouses now sell *Galanthus* green, but more commonly you'll have to find a gardener who's looking to divide his or her clump.

Galanthus elwesii

Q: I have heard about a flower called snowflake. Is this another name for snowdrops?

The Science Behind It: Snowdrops look somewhat like a flower called snowflake (also known as spring snowflakes), but snowflake is actually the common name for another genus of spring-flowering bulbs called *Leucojum*. Snowdrops and snowflakes both belong to the amaryllis family (*Amaryllidaceae*). In some parts of the world *Leucojum* is commonly referred to as snowdrops, but this is actually a misnomer.

Although the flowers of both genera have six petals, in *Galanthus* the three outer petals are significantly larger than the inner three; in some species, the inner petals are almost concealed. In *Leucojum* the six petals are roughly the same size and resemble little bells. *Leucojum* also bear up to eight flowers per stem, whereas *Galanthus* flowers are produced singly. *Leucojum* is also a bit taller than snowdrops, reaching 22–30 cm. It flowers a little later, usually anytime from the end of April through to early June. *Leucojum* naturalizes well, but is not quite as hardy as *Galanthus*, perennializing in Zones 4–10.

Gladiolus ❧ *Gladilous* x *hortulanus*

Q: When should I transplant my gladiolus corms into the garden?

Practical Advice: A general rule is to plant them as soon as the soil in your garden can be worked easily. The ground should have warmed to a depth of about 15 cm and the deciduous trees native to your area should have begun to leaf out.

Q: I want to have glads blooming in my garden all summer long. Is this possible?

Practical Advice: It's definitely possible, and well worth the effort. After you plant your first batch of corms, transplant more corms at one- to two-week intervals until early July. You should time your last set of transplants to coincide with the average date of the first killing frost in the fall. This timing will stretch the blooming season from a couple of weeks to almost two months: as one planting finishes flowering, the next should be starting to bloom. The number of days from planting to flowering ranges from 60 to 120, depending on the variety and size of the corms, your cultural practices and the weather during the growing season.

Q: What is the difference between miniature glads and baby glads?

The Science Behind It: *Miniature* glads are actually small-flowered varieties of the standard garden gladiolus. *Baby* glads are gladiolus varieties that have been developed from the *nanus* and *colveillei* species. Initially, baby glads were used almost exclusively in greenhouses for forcing as cutflowers. More recently, however, they have become popular as garden flowers.

Q: My glads look terrible! The plants are weak and the flowers don't last. What's the problem?

Practical Advice: The most likely problem is that your glad plants are over-fertilized. It's tempting to provide plants with lots of fertilizer, but with glads moderation is important: excessive fertilizer causes soft, weak growth, and the flowers deteriorate quickly, especially if they are used as cutflowers. Glads require the most water at the transplanting and flower spike development stages, which is also when they require the most nutrients. Be sure to provide fertilizer at these two periods.

Large-flowering gladiolus 'Semarang'

Butterfly gladiolus 'Shocking'

Gladiolus primulinus *'Columbine'*

116

The Science Behind It: Use a good-quality, balanced fertilizer. A granular all-purpose fertilizer can be mixed in at transplanting and then applied again as side dressing when the flower spikes begin to develop. Otherwise, apply a liquid transplanting fertilizer when you plant the corms, and fertilize once a week from the time flower spikes are initiated until the flowers are blooming.

Q: A friend of mine said you have specific advice for watering glads. What is it?

Practical Advice: I recommend watering glads at soil level. Drip irrigation or a soaker hose is best, since these methods provide water directly to where it is needed. You can also use a hose, but keep the nozzle close to the soil. Overhead watering can damage the flowers, causing spotting on the petals; it also splashes soil on the leaves and can promote the spread of disease.

The Science Behind It: Gladioli grow best with a good water supply. Although they will tolerate drier conditions than many other bulbs, lack of water will inhibit the development of the flower spikes, florets and new corms. Adequate moisture is essential at planting time because it promotes the development of a healthy, robust root system; it is especially important for late plantings because late-spring and early-summer conditions are drier and typically warmer than those in the early spring. Water is also very important when the flower spikes are first formed and when the florets begin to open.

Large-flowering gladiolus 'Breedsville'

The good rule for watering glads is to provide 3 cm of water each week. Be sure this water soaks into the ground and does not merely run off the surface.

Q: What are giant glads?

The Science Behind It: Giant glads are gladiolus varieties whose largest florets are 14 cm in diameter or larger. The other retail sizes of gladiolus are large (12–14 cm), medium (9–12 cm), small (6–9 cm) and miniature (less than 6 cm).

Large-flowering gladiolus 'Ramona'

117

Hyacinth 'Festival Blue'

Garden Hyacinths ∽ *Hyacinthus orientalis*

Q: Can you suggest a method for propagating hyacinth bulbs quickly?

The Science Behind It: Unlike many bulbs, hyacinths are slow to reproduce naturally. The best method for propagating hyacinth bulbs quickly is called scoring (also known as cross-cutting). The process can be time consuming, but it is not difficult. You will need a sunroom, small greenhouse or cold-frame because the light inside your house is insufficient. You also need to be patient because the process takes about four years from seeding to flower production.

In mid to late summer, after the foliage has stopped growing but before it has died down, dig up the bulbs. Make an incision in the shape of a cross on the basal plate of each bulb. Remove a thin sliver of the basal plate, ensuring that you do not cut into the main body of the bulb itself (the soft fleshy part). Plant the bulbs in a low, wide container or flat filled with high-quality potting mix. Once the leaves have died down completely, lift the bulb and you will see many tiny bulbils growing along the incisions on the basal plate. Carefully remove the bulbils and set them in trays to grow. They will reach flowering size in three to four years. It's best to wear gloves when working with hyacinths because the outer skins of the bulbs can cause skin irritations that make your hands very itchy and red.

Another propagation method is called scooping. It's a more complicated process than scoring and is rarely used by home gardeners; it's used by commercial growers to propagate large quantities of hyacinth bulbs. Scooping produces numerous smaller bulbs, but the bulbs still take three or four years to reach flowering size.

Q: I planted some hyacinth bulbs in my garden about five years ago. They have begun to naturalize, but now the flowers growing in my garden don't look the same as the ones I first planted. What's wrong?

Practical Advice: A common complaint of gardeners is that after a few years their hyacinths produce smaller flowers in smaller spikes. Your bulbs have probably become overcrowded; dividing them will help.

The Science Behind It: There are two tips that may extend the life of your naturalized hyacinths. The first is to plant the bulbs a bit deeper than recommended. The thinking here is that the soil stays cooler, so the bulb produces fewer but stronger bulbils. The bulbils compete for nutrients but never gain enough size to produce large flower spikes of full-size flowers. The second tip is to plant the bulbs in a location that is sunny in the spring but doesn't get too hot during the summer. In any case, you will need to renew hyacinths every few years.

Q: I have seen some hyacinths forced indoors in pots. I would like to try forcing some hyacinth bulbs myself. Is this hard to do?

Practical Advice: Hyacinths are among the earliest blooming spring-flowering bulbs when they are forced. Here's a method you can use with varieties suitable for indoor forcing.

1. Fill pots ⅔ full of high-quality potting soil.

2. Place the bulbs in the pots, spacing them so they are just far enough apart that they do not touch. For the best effect, plant bulbs singly or in odd-numbered groups. (I like to grow bulbs of the same variety in the same pot for strong *Wow!* effect. I prefer not to mix varieties because they tend to flower at different times.)

3. Add just enough mix to cover most of the bulb and leave the just the tip of the bulb protruding above the soil.

4. Move the pots to a cool, dark place where the temperature does not exceed 7–10°C. The fridge is a good choice; the garage is too, as long as it isn't kept too warm.

5. Keep the soil moist but not wet. Do not let the soil dry out; otherwise, the roots of the hyacinth bulbs will shrivel and die and the top growth will cease. A growing shoot should emerge within 12 to 15 weeks.

6. After the growing shoot has reached 4–5 cm and the flower buds are just beginning to show colour, remove the pots from the cool temperature and move them into a bright, indirect-light location where the temperature is about 18°C. Hyacinths will tolerate a warmer room but prefer to be kept cool.

7. After flowering, the bulbs will be exhausted and should be thrown away.

The Science Behind It: For an extended display, plant pots of bulbs every couple of weeks between September and mid December. The best display will come from size 18+ or 18/19 bulbs; large bulbs produce large, showy flowers.

For a list of the best hyacinth varieties for forcing, see page 60.

Q: I planted some hyacinth bulbs in pots to force indoors. When they flowered, the flowers were short and did not elongate properly. What did I do wrong?

The Science Behind It: This is a common problem that people experience when they try to force hyacinths indoors. It is generally easily corrected. Here is a list of the possible causes of this problem.

Hyacinth 'Festival Pink'

- The bulbs were brought into a warm, bright location prematurely. The shoots should be 3–5 cm high before they are exposed to light.
- The soil was allowed to dry out during some stage of forcing.
- The bulbs were grown too cold.
- Certain hyacinth cultivars are better suited to forcing than others. Stick with cultivars that are recommended for forcing, such as 'Pink Pearl', 'Delft Blue', 'Anne Marie' and 'Carnegie'. 'Hollyhock' is a good double-flowering variety for forcing.

Bluebells
Hyacinthoides spp.

Q: I have both English (*Hyacinthoides non-scripta*) and Spanish bluebells (*Hyacinthoides hispanica*) planted in my garden. Over the years, I'm finding it hard to tell which is which. Can you help?

Practical Advice: The two bluebells are quite similar, but there are a few visual clues that will help you tell them apart. Spanish bluebells are hardier and taller than the English bluebells. Their flower stems are more erect and do not nod at the tip. The individual blooms are more open and widely bell-shaped. They also produce larger, broader leaves. English bluebells produce flowers on one side of the flower stalk, whereas Spanish bluebells produce their blooms on both sides of the raceme.

The Science Behind It: When planted in the same area, Spanish and English bluebells often hybridize, leading to plants that display characteristics of both species. By now you probably have both species and some hybridized plants in your garden. Regardless, you end up with a beautiful patch of bluebells, and they are breathtaking in the spring.

Hyacinths forced in soil

121

Hyacinthoides hispanica

Q: I know that bluebells are true bulbs, but when I went to transplant mine they looked more like little potato tubers and I was having a difficult time identifying which end was up. Help!

Practical Advice: You're right. Bluebells are true bulbs, but they lack the papery protective tunic of most true bulbs. This tunic not only keeps the bulbs from drying out but makes it easier for the novice gardener to tell which end is up. If you look carefully, you should be able to locate the growing point or tip at the centre of the bulb. The fleshy layers that make up the bulb come together at this point. This is the top of the bulb and should point upwards when you transplant it into the garden. At the base of the bulb the layers are held together by a basal plate, which is the bottom of the bulb.

The good news is that if you do happen to transplant the bulb on its side, it will still grow; however, it will take extra energy from the bulb to correct the problem and possibly result in smaller flowers, a shorter blooming time, and a weaker plant. Best to plant right side up if you can!

122

Q: A friend of mine has a perennial in her garden that she refers to as Virginian bluebells. Can I get bulbs for this bluebell at my local garden centre?

The Science Behind It: *Bluebell* is the common name for a number of different flowers. Using Latin names helps avoid this problem. The plant you refer to is not actually a bulb at all, but a perennial called *Mertensia virginica*, also known as *M. pulmonarioides*. It is native to North America and can be grown from bare roots or cuttings. It produces tube-like flowers, 2–2.5 cm long, on 45-cm stems. The flowers start out pink, and then turn sky-blue and eventually indigo.

Bulbous Irises ✣ *Iris* spp.

Q: I bought a little pot of *Iris danfordiae* from a garden centre. Will they flower again next year?

Practical Advice: They will not flower again in the pot, but you can transfer them to the garden. After the irises have finished flowering, keep them watered and in the sunniest location possible until you can plant them out into your garden. Plant them about 15 cm deep in a full-sun location in your yard. They may flower next spring, or you may need to wait another year for new blooms.

Iris danfordiae

The Science Behind It: Irises are described as *shy* bulbs, which means that the bulbs are mature when they flower. After they have finished flowering, the bulbs divide into numerous smaller bulbs that are not large enough to flower the following season. However, a little patience will be rewarded. Leave the bulbs undisturbed and in a couple of years you will have a beautiful little clump of irises blooming in your garden. Because the bulbs split when they flower, you will soon have some bulbs flowering and some bulbs growing each season.

Q: What are the xiphium irises?

Practical Advice: This group of irises is commonly called the Dutch irises; they are also known as Spanish irises. Interestingly, despite their common name, the plants were never native to Holland. They are the product of breeding by the Dutch bulb company Van Tubergen and are widely grown commercially as cutflowers. The many named cultivars are widely recognized by florists and others in the commercial cutflower business.

The Science Behind It: Xiphium irises are about 60 cm in height and require full sun. They grow best in Zones 8 and 9 in rich, well-drained soil and are somewhat more prone to disease than are other irises. They typically flower in late spring and early summer. The flower colours range from light to dark blue, light to dark purple, yellow, and nearly pure white. There are also many bicoloured cultivars. The flowers are beautiful, but to me they are best enjoyed as cutflowers. I prefer the German and Japanese irises in my flower garden and the little species irises in my rock garden. They're tougher and more reliable than Xiphium irises.

Siberian Lily ✺ *Ixiolirion* spp.

Q: I saw some pretty little purple flowers blooming in my neighbour's yard this past spring. He told me that they were a type of iris, but when I tried to look them up in a book to find more information they were listed as *Ixiolirion tataricum*. Which information is right?

Practical Advice: Both sources are partly right. This little bulb was formerly classified as either *Iris montanum* or *Iris pallasii*; you will still find it listed under these names in some references. Recently, however, it has been reclassified into a group of its own: *Ixiolirion tataricum*, in the amaryllis family *(Amaryllidaceae)*.

The Science Behind It: *I. tataricum* has grass-like leaves and star-shaped flowers. The flower colour tends to be light purple and the final plant height is 40–50 cm, quite a bit taller than the little species irises. The plant requires more sun than irises do and does not tolerate shade. It likes dry soil, so do not plant it in areas of your garden where the soil stays moist all season or is poorly drained. *I. tataricum* typically flowers in late May and early June. It can be used in areas of your rock garden where the plants are a bit taller. It is a good choice for borders and mixed flowerbeds, and makes an excellent, short-lived cutflower. It is hardy to Zone 4, but will survive in Zone 3 with winter protection. It naturalizes in Zones 4–7, but slowly.

Muscari ⚘ *Muscari* spp.

Q: What is the difference between grape hyacinths and hyacinths?

The Science Behind It: Grape hyacinth is a common name for muscari, but this species is distinct from the true hyacinths (*Hyacinthus* spp.)— although the plants are related. Most muscari species produce blooms with constricted mouths; this characteristic is the main feature that distinguishes muscari from true hyacinths, whose flowers have wide open and often flared mouths. Muscari flowers are also much smaller than hyacinth flowers. Muscari flowers come primarily in shades of blue and purple, with some white cultivars. True hyacinth flowers come in a much wider range of colours, including white, yellow, orange, pink, blue, purple and even red.

Interestingly, one of the muscari species used to be classified with the hyacinths: *M. azureum* was formerly *Hyacinthus azureus*.

Muscari armeniacum *'Blue Spike'*

Q: What is the difference between *Muscari comosum* and *M. comosum* 'Plumosum'?

The Science Behind It: The short answer is *M. comosum* 'Plumosum' (commonly known as feather hyacinth) is a cultivar of *M. comosum* (commonly known as tassel grape hyacinth). Tassel grape hyacinth grows about 20–25 cm tall with unusual feathery flowers. The flowers of feather hyacinth are taller and are actually sterile branched purple flower stems. The true flowers appear lower on the flower stalk a few weeks after the false blooms.

Q: I planted some muscari bulbs this fall and they have already produced foliage. I'm worried that they'll die over the winter. Have I done something wrong? Why did they do this?

Practical Advice: Don't be alarmed. Some species of muscari form clumps of leaves in the fall. They will survive just fine over the winter, and new growth will emerge in the spring from these clumps without causing any problems.

The Science Behind It: *Muscari armeniacum* is more prone to producing fall foliage than other muscari species. Naturalized clumps of grape hyacinth also tend to produce late foliage. The leaves may show frost damage in the spring, which manifests as brown tips on the ends of the leaves, and the damage remains visible during the flowering period. It can be unsightly, but it does not harm the bulbs. The flowers are rarely affected and will bloom normally.

Muscari azureum

Q: I forced some muscari bulbs in pots indoors. Will they rebloom? Can I plant them in the garden?

Practical Advice: After the first bloom has finished, the bulbs will often send up more flower spikes, so don't be in a hurry to toss the pots after the first bloom is done. The spent bulbs can be planted in the garden as soon as the ground is workable. After the flowers have finished, keep the pot well watered and leave it in indirect light until the weather warms up. Plant the bulbs 5–10 cm deep and keep them well watered. Be sure to leave the foliage intact—it nourishes the bulbs and will eventually die back. Next spring, your muscari will rebloom in the garden.

Muscari botryoides
'Album'

Narcissus ♫ *Narcissus* spp.

Q: What is the difference between a narcissus and a daffodil?

Practical Advice: The short answer is that there is no difference. *Narcissus* and *daffodil* are synonyms. *Narcissus* is the Latin name for daffodil. *Daffodil* is the common name for all members of the genus *Narcissus*.

The Science Behind It: Another common name is jonquil, but this one is trickier: a jonquil is always a narcissus but a narcissus isn't always a jonquil. The term has been used incorrectly to refer to any yellow daffodil. However, the general rule is that jonquil species and their hybrids share certain common characteristics: they have more than one flower per stem, a strong fragrance and rounded foliage. The term *jonquil* should be used only when referring to Division 7 narcissus or to Division 10 cultivars that are known to belong to the jonquil group.

Trumpet narcissus 'King Alfred'

127

Q: What is a paperwhite? Is it actually a narcissus?

Practical Advice: Yes. Paperwhites belong to the Tazetta group of narcissus. They are primarily sold for forcing indoors and can easily be brought into bloom for the winter holidays. They can also be grown outside in very mild zones (Zones 9 and 10).

Q: My daffodils bloomed well for a number of seasons but have gradually produced fewer and fewer blooms. This spring they produced hardly any flowers. What could the problem be?

The Science Behind It: It sounds like a case of *blindness*. This term is used when daffodils fail to produce flowers. The problem is usually overcrowding. How long a clump takes to become overcrowded depends on the vigour of the variety and how closely the original bulbs were planted.

Every year or two the original bulb splits in two. Given the right conditions, this pattern will repeat itself year after year until eventually the clump becomes overcrowded. As long as adequate light, water, nutrients and soil oxygen are available the bulbs will continue to grow, but eventually they may cease to produce flowers. The best flowers are generally produced the second, third or fourth year; afterward, the flowers gradually become smaller and less numerous. Overcrowding is generally a problem with larger-flowered cultivars. Small-flowered daffodils and species narcissus continue to flower well even when they are congested.

Trumpet narcissus 'Spellbinder'

Large-cupped narcissus 'Flower Record'

Q: I planted some daffodils in my garden and they have been growing poorly for a couple of years now. I dug some up to check the bulbs and found many infested with maggots. Can you tell me what kind of maggot this is and what I can do to control it?

The Science Behind It: I hope you're not squeamish! The insect you describe sounds like the larva of the narcissus bulb fly, *Merodon equestris*. It was originally introduced to North America from Europe in the mid 1800s. The adult flies are about 1 cm long with brown bodies; they resemble small honey bees. These flies attack members of the amaryllis family, which includes daffodils. The narcissus bulb fly is an uncommon pest, so you may want to take a sample to your local garden centre for verification.

Once you have confirmed the problem, you must be vigilant to control the insect. The fly lays its eggs in the spring in the crown of the plant. The maggots work their way down into the bulb and eat it, hollowing out the centre. The bulb then rots, causing weak, yellow growth and foliage that is almost grass-like in appearance.

If your daffodils are infected, dig up all the bulbs in late spring and destroy all those that are obviously infected. Infected bulbs feel soft, mushy or spongy. Do not put them in your compost pile. Store healthy bulbs in a cool, dry location with good air circulation until the end of the summer.

Recheck the bulbs for signs of infestation. Look for holes in the bulb or soft, hollow bulb necks that feel soft when squeezed. You may also notice a very small white growth, about the size of a pea, at the base of the bulb. Discard and destroy any bulbs with these symptoms; they are likely infected with narcissus bulb fly. Replant healthy bulbs in the garden in the fall, but continue to monitor for problems.

If this seems like a lot of work, simply throw out the clumps of infected bulbs and purchase new ones in the fall.

Q: I live in Zone 8. I love daffodils, but I've heard they're hard to grow successfully in areas where the ground doesn't freeze. What should I do?

Practical Advice: Don't despair; there are three divisions of daffodils that will grow successfully in your area: cyclamineus daffodils, tazetta daffodils and jonquilla daffodils. You can also try any variety that is listed as "early," because the earlier-flowering varieties tend to grow more successfully in very warm climates than do the later-flowering varieties. These varieties require a cool period of two to three months (with night temperatures below 5°C), but the cold doesn't have to be severe. In the very warmest zones, stick to the tazetta types. Paperwhites, from the tazetta group, don't require a chilling period at all.

The Science Behind It: The most important factor to keep in mind when planting is to choose an area where there is adequate moisture and the soil is well drained. Daffodils do not like soggy soil when they are dormant. If the ground stays wet the bulbs will rot, especially in warmer temperatures. Plant your daffodils in a raised bed, where the drainage is superior, or in a container. Never plant them in an area of the garden that has automatic irrigation.

Oxalis ‿ *Oxalis* spp.

Q: A friend gave me a good luck clover, which I have been growing in my kitchen. Lately the leaves have been getting thinner and less colourful. What's wrong?

Practical Advice: The plant you're describing is *Oxalis deppei*. It prefers well-drained, sandy soil and full sun. It may be that your plant is not receiving enough direct light. Try moving it to a brighter, sunnier spot. Keep in mind that good luck clover is sold with several bulbs in each pot, and they can become overcrowded quickly. You can divide the clump, replant a few bulbs and pass on the extras to a friend. This should bring back your good luck!

Puschkinia scilloides

Puschkinias ∿ *Puschkinia* spp.

Q: What is the difference between chionodoxas and puschkinias?

The Science Behind It: Like chionodoxas, puschkinias have a short tube and a cone of stamens. In puschkinias, the filaments are flattened and joined together to make a small corona in the centre of each flower. Puschkinias have two leaves and a short flower stalk with up to 15 slightly bell-shaped flowers. Each flower is 1 to 1.5 cm long. Most chionodoxa flowers are a bit larger, from 1.5 to 4 cm across, depending upon the species. The most common puschkinia species has dark-blue vertical stripes on each petal; these stripes are not found on chionodoxa flowers. Most chionodoxa flowers have a white centre, while puschkinia flowers are solidly coloured.

Q: Are *Puschkinias* actually *Scillas?* I've seen them both referred to as squills. What is the difference?

The Science Behind It: There is only one *Puschkinia* species, correctly named *P. scilloides,* but it is often listed under a number of synonyms, most typically *P. libanotica. Puschkinias* and *Scillas* are related, and both are often confused with both chionodoxas (*Chionodoxa* spp.) and Siberian squills (*Scilla siberica*). Puschkinias are distinguished from chionodoxas by their fused flower filaments and from Siberian squills by their six petals, which are fused at the base.

Squills ⌇ *Scilla* spp.

Q: What is the difference between *Chionodoxa* and *Scilla*?

The Science Behind It: *Scilla* species, commonly called squills, produce bright-blue flowers early in the spring: flowers can be bell-shaped or star-shaped, and are produced on long erect flower stems. Each stem can bear anywhere from a few to many individual blooms. Each flower has six petals that are split right to the base of the flower. In *Chionodoxa* species, the petals are joined at the base of the flower, forming a tube. *Scilla* flowers have wide-spreading stamens, while the stamens in *Chionodoxa* flowers are tightly grouped, resembling a thick central tube in each flower. Most chionodoxa flowers also have a white eye.

Blue is the most common flower colour for both squills and chinodoxas, but as a result of breeding there are now purple, white and pink squill cultivars, and pink and white chionodoxa cultivars.

Scilla mischtschenkoana

Q: What is the difference between squills and striped squills? Are they the same species?

The Science Behind It: This distinction is always a bit confusing, and the problem is due to common names. Striped squill is actually the common name for a bulb species called *Puschkinia scilloides* var. *libanotica*. This species produces pale-blue bell-shaped flowers. Squill is also the common name for several early-flowering bulbs in the genus *Scilla*, including the most common squill, *S. siberica*, and its cultivars, as well as *S. bifolia*, *S. pratensis* and *S. mischtschenkoana*. Squills and puschkinias are closely related and are also related to chionodoxa—you could call them first cousins!

Q: What is the difference between wood hyacinths and hyacinths? I've seen wood hyacinths listed as both hyacinths and *Scillas*.

The Science Behind It: Wood hyacinth (*S. campanulata*, also known as *S. hispanica*) is correctly classified with the squills. Contrary to what you might think, not all *Scilla* species are referred to as squills. *S. nutans* (also known as *S. non-scripta*) is commonly called English bluebells, and *S. peruviana* has the common name Cuban lily.

Just to add to the confusion, English bluebell and Spanish bluebell, two of the later-flowering *Scillas*, have recently been reclassified under genus *Hyacinthoides*. Most bulb companies and catalogues still list these bulbs with the *Scillas* because that's where most people look for them. However, many specialty mail-order catalogues are starting to list them under hyacinths, and I believe they will eventually be grouped with the hyacinths.

Scilla siberica

Scilla siberica alba

Darwin tulip 'Blushing Apeldoorn'

Tulips ～ *Tulipa* spp.

Q: What is the key to maintaining good tulips year after year?

Practical Advice: It's easy! Provide good growing conditions so the plants produce the largest, healthiest daughter bulbs possible. Plant the tulips in the best location in your garden, with well-drained soil and lots of sun. The sun is critical to photosynthesis, which creates the energy that is stored in the daughter bulbs. Always allow tulip leaves to die down naturally. Inexperienced gardeners often remove the foliage prematurely because it can look unsightly, but healthy tulips need prolonged exposure to the sun. If the daughter bulbs are big and full, they will produce large, beautiful flowers the following year.

The Science Behind It: Finally, hope for a cool summer; if the season is too hot, the bulbs will not grow to their full potential. There's a reason that coastal B.C., coastal Washington state, and Holland are major bulb producers: they tend to have relatively cool summers that are just the right temperature for optimum leaf development and the production of large bulbs.

Tulips will also benefit from fertilizer after they flower. Mix granular bulb food into the soil around the base of the plant or apply liquid 10-52-10 fertilizer. The best hybrid tulips for reblooming are Darwin hybrids and the botanicals (*T. fosteriana, T. greigii* and *T. kaufmanniana*).

134

Q: Realistically, how long can I expect my hybrid tulips to rebloom reliably?

Practical Advice: Most hybrid tulips will re-bloom fairly reliably for three to five years given proper care: adequate moisture, a sunny location with good drainage and a complete growth cycle (i.e., the foliage is allowed to dry and die down). However, some categories of tulips are far better suited to reblooming than others. The best hybrid tulips for reblooming are Darwin hybrids and the botanicals (*T. fosteriana, T. greigii* and *T. kaufmanniana*).

Q: What's with all the different types of tulips? How do I know which ones to buy?

The Science Behind It: There are in fact 15 separate classifications of tulip cultivars, each displaying distinct characteristics. By grouping cultivars that share similar characteristics, grow-ers have made it at least a little easier for con-sumers to choose bulbs with the traits they desire.

For example, if you want tulips that have similar growth habits and bloom in succession, buy single early and single late tulips (Division 1 and 2 tulips, respectively). If you love frilly, ruffled petals, choose fringed (Division 7) or parrot (Division 10) tulips. The classifications make it all-around easier to get what you want.

Q: What are tall tulips?

Practical Advice: Everything's relative, but the general rule is that any tulip whose height ex-ceeds 60 cm is considered to be tall. Most of the tall varieties are in the Darwin hybrid and single late groups—some single late varieties can reach 75 cm! There are also some taller varieties in the fringed, lily-flowered, parrot and triumph groups.

Fragrant Tulips

Hybrid tulips
'Ad Em' (Darwin) • Scarlet-edged with yellow
'Allegretto' (double late) • Red with yellow edges
'Angelique' (double late) • Pale- and dark-pink tones
'Apricot Parrot' (parrot) • Apricot-pink with green stripes
'Ballerina' (lily-flowered) • Bright orange
'Christmas Dream' (single early) • Cherry-red
'Christmas Marvel' (single early) • Cherry-pink
'Couleur Cardinal' (single early) • Red
'Monte Carlo' (double early) • Yellow (my personal favourite for fragrance)
'Princess Irene' (triumph) • Orange and purple
'Rococo' (parrot) • Red with green-and-yellow ruffles
'Purissima' (fosteriana) • White

Species tulips
T. aucheriana
T. kolpakowskiana
T. sylvestris
T. tarda
T. urumiensis

Double early tulip 'Monte Carlo'

Ice tulips

Ice tulips, also called Eskimo tulips, are ordinary tulips subjected to a treatment that forces them to bloom in the late summer or early fall rather than in the spring. To create ice tulips, growers lift and store the bulbs until late October. They plant the bulbs in trays and store them at cold temperatures for four weeks. The trays are then wrapped and stored for a further nine months. After that time, the trays are moved to a greenhouse where they grow normally, producing flowers in late summer.

The procedure to create ice tulips was developed in 1977, chiefly so that cut tulips could be available in the off-season. The vase life of ice tulips is about the same as cut tulips grown using normal techniques.

Q: What are botanical tulips?

The Science Behind It: "Botanical tulip" is just a generic descriptor for species tulips. Species tulips are divided into groups according to their origin, and we refer to the cultivated varieties in this group as 'botanicals' for convenience. Most flower early in the spring and naturalize well. The group includes *T. greigii*, *T. fosteriana*, *T. kaufmanniana* and *T. praestans* as well as the various species tulips.

Q: I'd like to plant some wild tulips. Can you suggest some really hardy ones for my Zone 3 garden?

Practical Advice: There are more than 100 known species of wild tulips, and many are hardy to your zone. One of the differences between this group of tough little plants and their cousins the hybrids is that wild tulips do not like pampering! Give them a hot, dry location that is well drained and spacious enough that their foliage isn't covered or crowded by other plants.

The Science Behind It: Wild tulips are smaller, cost less at the garden centre and can be an integral part of a low-maintenance or xeriscape landscape. Species blooms vary significantly in

Greigii tulip 'Fur Elise' (above); Triumph tulip 'Red Lips' (right)

form, so you have an interesting array to choose from. Some of my favourites include *Tulipa acuminata*, *T. bakeri*, *T. batalinii*, *T. clusiana* var. *chrysantha*, *T. eichleri*, *T. humilis* and *T. tarda*, but there are many, many more—give them a try!

Q: I've seen catalogues list Darwin tulips and Darwin hybrid tulips. Are they the same?

Practical Advice: Darwin tulips are actually an older classification of a group now referred to as single late tulips. They have large flowers and long stems and flower in the late spring. Darwin hybrid tulips are tulips produced by hybridization between cultivars of the Darwin group and cultivars of the Fosteriana group. Darwin hybrids have the large flowers and strong stems of Fosteriana tulips, and the height and wide range of colours of the Darwin group. They bloom in mid spring, a happy compromise between the early spring blooms of the Fosteriana group and the late spring blooms of the Darwin group.

Q: Is there such a thing as a black tulip?

Practical Advice: I think it is innate in gardeners to want something unusual or different. Breeders have been trying to produce a black tulip for centuries, but there is still no truly black tulip available. Breeders have come very close, producing tulips that are deep maroon and dark burgundy. Here is a list of very dark tulips.
'Queen of the Night'(single late)
'Black Diamond' (single late)
'Black Hero' (double late)
'Burgundy' (lily-flowered)
'Black Parrot' (parrot)

Q: I want to create a garden with a Canadian theme. Are there any Canadian-bred tulips?

Practical Advice: The province of British Columbia grows a large number of tulip bulbs commercially for international breeders, but I'm not currently aware of any popular Canadian-bred tulips. However, many tulips are named for Canadian locations. Here are a few.

Darwin hybrids
'The Mounties'

Greigii varieties
'Orange Toronto'
'Quebec'
'Toronto'

Triumph varieties
'Calgary'
'Canada'
'Ottawa'

Single late varieties
'City of Vancouver'

Q: I've heard that many tulips have unusual leaves. Can you tell my what characteristics make the leaves different and which varieties have different leaves?

Practical Advice: Several tulip varieties have unusual leaves. Most of them belong to the botanical tulip groups *T. greigii*, *T. fosteriana* and *T. kaufmanniana*. Here is a list, including leaf characteristics.

T. fosteriana varieties
  'Gluck' • red and yellow flowers with broad, mottled leaves

T. greigii varieties
  'Cape Cod' • Yellow-edged apricot flowers with spotted leaves
  'Oratorio' • Rose-pink flowers with spotted leaves
  'Oriental Beauty' • Carmine-red flowers with spotted leaves
  'Plaisir' • White-edged carmine-red flowers with spotted leaves

T. praestans varieties
  'Unicum' • Multiple scarlet-red flowers per stem with distinctly yellow-edged leaves

T. kaufmanniana varieties
  'Heart's Delight' • Pink-edged carmine-red flowers with spotted foliage
  'Johann Strauss' • Soft-yellow-edged currant-red flowers with spotted foliage
  'Showwinner' • Cardinal-red flowers with spotted foliage
  'Stresa' • Red-and-yellow flowers with spotted foliage

Triumph varieties
  'Charmeur' • Red-and-white flowers with a distinct narrow cream edge on the leaves
  'New Design' • Pink flowers with a distinct white edge on the leaves

Q: One of my tulip flowers has developed unusual streaks on the petals. It is pretty but it looks very different from my other tulips and it also looks different than it did last year. Why would this happen?

The Science Behind It: If a single-coloured tulip suddenly sports stripes one spring, dig it up and destroy it. Tulip flowers that are flamed or whose flowers are stretched or distorted can be attractive, but the streaks indicate that the bulb has been infected with a virus. Viruses are spread by aphids and thrips, and if you don't remove and destroy the infected plant, all your tulips will eventually become infected. Virally infected plants do not grow as well as healthy plants and eventually die. The virus can also be spread to other bulbous plants like lilies and fritillaries. If you like the look of viral tulip flowers, purchase some Rembrandt tulips. These tulips are bred to look like the old, unhealthy varieties but are not actually infected with virus; they are healthy, vigorous bulbs.

Afterword

My attitude towards gardening is a little unusual. I'm not a fussy gardener; I don't mind if a flowerbed or container isn't letter-perfect. Nor do I tend to putter, spending hours trimming hedges or manicuring my lawn so that every blade is in place. I like a good-looking garden, but there's a limit to the amount of time and effort I'm willing to expend on it. In fact, if my plants are attacked by a particularly vicious disease or pest, I don't even consider it a complete disaster: I love to see how pests and plants interact. In fact, the interactions between all the various life forms in the garden can be downright fascinating.

I find bulbs especially fascinating. Every year we're inundated with brand new varieties—some beautiful, some bizarre, some with more subtle improvements such as increased weather tolerance or disease resistance. It's always interesting to see how these new varieties perform in different conditions. After my sister-in-law, Valerie, puts these bulbs through her yearly trials, there are always a few I'd gladly add to my garden, and others I wouldn't touch with a ten foot pole. But whether or not new bulbs satisfy my own performance criteria, they're all valuable in that they have something new to teach us. I enjoy bulb gardening not so much because the plants are beautiful—though they certainly are—but because I find their life cycles so interesting. We all get something different out of the garden, and for me it's the deep satisfaction that I get from discovering something new about plants. That's what keeps me gardening.

So Ask Us Some Questions...

We plan to update all of the *Question and Answer* books periodically. If you have a gardening question that's been troubling you, write to us! While we can't answer your inquiries individually, your question may appear in future *Q&A* books—along with the answer, naturally. And don't ever think that a question is "dumb" or "too simple." Odds are that any mysteries you face are shared by countless other gardeners.

Send your questions to:
Hole's Q&A Questions
101 Bellerose Drive
St. Albert, AB T8N 8N8
CANADA

You can also send us e-mail at *yourquestions@enjoygardening.com*,
or visit us at www.enjoygardening.com.

Index

Index